"Dirty
Northern
B*st*rds!"

"Dirty Northern B*st*rds!"

And Other Tales From The Terraces

The story of Britain's
FOOTBALL CHANTS

TIM MARSHALL

First published 2014
by Elliott and Thompson Limited
27 John Street
London WC1N 2BX
www.eandtbooks.com

ISBN: 978-1-78396-060-6

9 8 7 6 5 4

A catalogue record for this book is available from the British Library.
Typesetting by Marie Doherty

Printed in the UK by CPI Group (UK) Ltd, Croydon, CR0 4YY

Contents

Dedicated to Mickey Deane,
shot dead in Cairo, 14 August 2013.
Despite not being fussed about football, he was a great
photojournalist, and a wonderful lion of a man.

Introduction

This is a book about the wisdom of the masses, and the madness of the crowd. It's about football and Britain, and Britain and football, because you cannot fully understand one without the other. If you haven't got a sense of humour it's not worth even trying, as wit runs through both like the Clyde through Glasgow and the writing through a stick of Blackpool rock.

It's about people with a little education and a lot of intelligence, and vice versa. Unfortunately, it also has to be about people with little of either. Crucially, it's not supposed to be too serious, but at times you must bear with me – the songs and chants will start again. They always do.

My name's Tim Marshall and it's been a week since my last match. I support a football club. That's not just five words; it's a life sentence.

I came late to the game. You do hear some fans recounting how they first heard the roar of the crowd from within their mother's womb, aged minus four months. More plausibly, others will tell you about being hoisted onto their dad's shoulders, aged five, or being passed over the heads of fans to get to the front of the Kop, aged seven. I confess to being a johnny-come-lately ten-year-old when, armed only with a pair of Joe 90 NHS specs and an impressionable mind, I first clicked my way through a turnstile, mounted the concrete steps and emerged into another world.

It was love at first sight, and my first sight was at 2.30 p.m., Saturday, 18 April 1970.

The old adage 'The past is another country: they do things differently there' was only ever partially true – and so it is with football.

For the first few years, when I began going, the game was usually on a Saturday afternoon. The crowd was 90 per cent male in the standing areas and the ground would already have been half full an hour before the 3 o'clock kick-off. By then the singing would be well under way – the PA system didn't bother blasting pop music at us to distortion levels and things would build to a natural crescendo.

By 3 p.m. we were jammed together so tightly that it was difficult to turn around, as your shoulders would be pushing into the people each side of you and there was pressure from front and back. We never thought about these conditions. It was all we knew and, until Hillsborough, all we would know. Behind you there would be a surge of people and you would stagger down three or four steps, struggling to keep your footing, before surging back up the terraces, sometimes having moved across to the left or right by several feet.

The noise was deafening, wave upon wave of songs crashing along the terraces and surging out onto the pitch. The Kop at our ground held 17,000 people, the ground 50,000. Sometimes, in the second half, the PA would announce the attendance. When it came out as being in the 30,000s, and yet we could barely move for the crush, a knowing laugh would go up. It was cash at the gate and we always reckoned that the club, for obvious reasons, might want to knock a few thousand off the attendance figures.

Those were also the days when two of you could push through the turnstile together as long as the guy taking the money got something out of it. Another way of getting in was to slip some money to the man on the sliding gate at the end of the stand. In extremis, you could try to crawl through your friend's legs while he fiddled for the right money to give you time to get through the turnstile, but this often ended with a bruised forehead and deep embarrassment when the turnstile man looked down and said, 'What you doing down there, lad?' In that event you'd have to go along to the next turnstile and try again.

If the stand behind the goal was sold out, you could try the most difficult trick. Pay the cheaper price for the family section along the side of the pitch, work your way to near the corner flag, then jump over the barrier, sprint across the grass, and dive into the Kop. If you made it, the crowd would part, you would disappear, ducking down as it closed behind you and you worked your way up to where you might, or might not, find your friends. The stewards didn't really care and the police had better things to do than push through hundreds of people in order to catch you.

Try doing that in an all-seater stadium these days. You'd never make it to the stand and you'd probably then be arrested and banned for life. I'm not defending my various attempts to defraud my club of money, and will be happy to send a cheque for the £5 or so I might have saved over my first few years of attending. But in that culture you didn't think of these practices as wrong, and certainly not as breaking the law. You just chanced it. If you got away with it – fine. If you didn't – no harm done.

As a young teenager you were stuck more or less in the same spot once the game began. The old stories of the terraces running with urine are true. I never saw anyone 'piss in your pocket', and think that commonly told tale is a myth, but it wasn't unusual to head across to the nearest pillar holding up the stadium roof and urinate against it. To get from near the back of the Kop to the toilets under the stand was a twenty-minute battle many of us didn't bother fighting. Most of the older, bigger guys would push their way through the crowd to reach the urinals, but people would often refuse to move for a scrawny teenager. When you reached a stanchion, the wall of legs in front of you was impossible to duck under or through.

None of this mattered. It was part of the day and it was about the team. I was lucky – supporting one of the biggest clubs in Europe during a successful period. The crowds were huge, the atmosphere febrile. There would be lads standing on the stanchions leading the singing, with just about everyone behind the goal joining in, their 17,000 voices making a wall of noise. That's when and where I first felt that community spirit, that sense of singleness of purpose, diamond-sharp focus and sheer energy.

All this was replicated on the pitch. The passion for the game was intense, the skills at the highest levels. As young schoolboys, our version of football was to kick the ball, and then run after it. Suddenly I was confronted with passing systems, marking, tactics and creating space. I was dazzled at the patterns being woven across the pitch. It was breathtaking to see one player run five yards with no intention of receiving the ball, but take a defender with him and thus leave a gap for a team mate to run into. This was the beautiful game. When I came across Johan Cruyff's adage that 'football is a game you play with your brain', the whole thing fell into place. If you doubt the Dutch master's word, then watch a top team, in arrogant cruise control at two–nil up, turn into panicked Sunday leaguers if it goes to two–one with fifteen minutes to go. It happens every time.

I came from a family of staunch Methodists, a religion and community I still admire, although as a child I felt stifled by a blanket of non-conformist conformity. Humour and passion are not high on the list of Methodist traits, but now I had found a place where the opposite was true and where revelation was not just a book in the Bible. Soon I was going week in, week out, home and away. I learned more about the geography of Britain from travelling to games than I ever did at the comprehensive school I occasionally frequented. It was the same for all the guys I went with. We all finished our education at sixteen with a thorough grasp of where Coventry is, and where West Ham were in the league table (towards the bottom usually), but little else.

For that the blame lies partly with us for our behaviour and partly with the school. Those years taught me a valuable lesson – the difference between education and intelligence; if you have intelligence, and can be motivated, then you can be taught.

We were self taught because we were motivated. We knew the name of every single one of the ninety-two league clubs. We knew their nicknames, their managers, the names of their stadiums, where they were in the leagues, how many games they had left. We could calculate how many points club X would need to avoid relegation if club Y won two more games and what the goal difference was for each. We knew who had won the FA Cup and League

Championship for each of the past twenty seasons. If there had been GSCEs in football facts, we would all have got straight As.

I've kept the lesson all my life. Your social background is not the determining factor in your abilities or knowledge, and your intelligence can be better judged by what you say than how you say it. You may find these truths to be self evident, but I am not convinced that, in our class-ridden and increasingly status-obsessed society, this is evident to everyone. There is snobbery towards football fans and players to a degree not seen in other sports.

This brings us back to why the past is only partly another country. Sure, we do things differently now, but at heart, it's the same – in some ways better, in some ways worse, but the same.

The flow of people heading in the same direction, the camaraderie in the pubs, the clicking of the turnstiles, the communal singing, the sense of purpose, the loyalty: it's all the same in spirit if not in detail. Oh, and the game – that's more or less the same as well. The ball is still round and the objective is still to get it into the goal, even if at times that's hard to believe. The tactics are now more complex, but it's still a simple game and it's still the beautiful game.

When my publishers asked why I wanted to write this book I was at first caught out, then stumped, but I recovered in time to remember that I wanted to write a book about football and not cricket. So, here it is.

PMT
(Pre Match Tension)

It starts with one voice, one word. Within a second, hundreds of people hear it. By the third word they are joining in. The song tumbles down the terraces, spreads across to left and right, and by the end of the first line it is one voice again, only this time there are thousands combining as one.

And with it comes that unity of purpose, of belonging, of identity, tradition, history – and the unspoken knowledge that without it, the reality it creates would vanish.

Without this, the cameras would never come, the working-class multi-millionaires from the Mersey, the Thames, and the Tyne, now glittering like stars across stadiums and TV screens the world over, would go back to their housing estates, and the dazzling skills of the boys from Brazil would shine only in the favelas.

Imagine a Premier League match played without a crowd. It's the football equivalent of the old Buddhist question: never mind whether a tree would make a sound if it fell in a forest but no one heard it; if Ronaldo scored in an empty stadium, would it still be a goal?

The tales we tell each other on the terraces create something you cannot see, only feel, but it is very real and it goes very deep. In our great stadiums, week in, week out, an atmosphere is created. From the four corners of the country people pour into the four corners of the theatre. Sometimes at night the green of the pitch is so brilliant in the glare of the floodlights that it almost hurts, and nothing exists apart from the great game. The night sky is erased behind the lights, outside the world stops, the worries of every-day life are gone, and all eyes are drawn to the magical field upon which dreams are played.

But let's not forget . . . this togetherness, this depth of purpose and unity? It's also a right laugh.

Football Chants in Britain Today

It's cold, wet and muddy. Perfect conditions for Chelsea v. Newcastle on a Saturday afternoon in late February at Stamford Bridge.

The Chelsea midfield genius, Bobby von Dazzler, five foot six of pure talent, is busy sashaying through the Newcastle defence – the term 'silky skills' is being used by the talkSPORT commentator – when suddenly the Newcastle centre half enforcer, Ernst Strongman, six foot six of solid oak, decides 'that's quite enough of that': a tree trunk of leg scythes down the gazelle. The injured party utters a scream that can be heard in row Z, collapses like Bambi on ice and then rolls over four times, which is three times too many for a real injury, but one less than is required for even the home fans to start laughing at the acting skills.

And then from the Shed End comes the chant: 'You dirty northern bastards! – You dirty northern bastards!'

By now the beautiful game is heading towards World Wrestling slam-down levels of theatricality. Ernst has both hands at his head, then palms outstretched in an 'I never touched him' gesture and, finally, a look of sheer incredulity on his face when the referee blows for a foul. (This can progress to holding one's head in both hands and even sinking to one's knees at the injustices of life if a yellow card is produced.) Ernst's team mates are by now either surrounding the referee, wagging their fingers in a 'no, no, no' manner and pointing to other parts of the pitch where various alleged transgressions have taken place without such punishment, or are holding their foreheads against their rivals' foreheads as though trying for a part in a new TV wildlife programme. At least one goalkeeper will race towards the mêlée to act as peacekeeper and then get involved in a pushing match with a player, possibly one from his own team.

Von Dazzler is still on the floor holding various parts of his anatomy, including his head, even though it had been a yard above the tackle. Unless restrained by the club doctor he may still get the odd roll or two in.

Four slightly overweight men in yellow fluorescent jackets have appeared on the pitch carrying a stretcher and are accompanied by an anxious-looking woman from the St John's Ambulance Brigade. At this point the Newcastle fans, 100 yards away at the other end of the pitch, will have convinced themselves that Ernst never touched Bobby and so break into the correct response to the 'Dirty northern bastards!' chant, which is: 'Soft southern bastard! You're just a soft southern bastard!' This is based on the belief that even if Ernst had shot Bobby with a Kalashnikov rifle, Bobby should still just get up and get on with the game, because that's what a northerner would do.

The Newcastle fans, to a man, woman and bairn, are 100 per

cent sure about the iniquity of the home team and their tendency to cheat. It is 20/20 vision, rock solid clear to all of them that von Dazzler had not been fouled. Even the ones who had been under the stand buying an overpriced meat pie know for a fact that it was a fair tackle because their mate told them so when they got back to their seat.

Now, ignore for a moment that Soft-Southern-Bastard Bobby might actually be from the Netherlands, which is slightly to the north of Chelsea, and that Dirty-Northern-Bastard Ernst hails from Nigeria, which is south of the King's Road. What is important here is the Industrial Revolution.

The broad-brush reality of the nineteenth and twentieth centuries has left us with a residue of the idea that the North is the land of coal fields, ship-building, steel factories, rows of red-brick two-up-two-downs and dark satanic mills as far as the smoke-filled eye can see. Think Lowry, the Jarrow March and *Coronation Street*.

The South, meanwhile, is awash with stockbrokers in country mansions who live up the hill from a million characterless Barratt houses inhabited by people who, to a man and a woman, vote Tory and dream of escaping to the country. Counties such as Wiltshire, Devon and Dorset do not appear in this mental map of the south. There are a few cheeky chappies dotted around as well, but they are all down the Queen Vic wearing coats festooned with pearls and asking each other if anyone wants to buy a motor. Think the Chelsea Flower Show, *To the Manor Born*, *EastEnders* and *Only Fools and Horses*.

The modern realities of the north and south need not trouble us once we enter a football stadium, or indeed any conversation about football; the old stereotypes are much more satisfying and lend themselves to far better, indeed funnier, chants.

So, by signing for Chelsea, or indeed any club south of Leicester, honorary soft southerner status is conferred, and honorary dirty northern bastard is conferred on anyone signing for a team north of Peterborough. Between Leicester and Peterborough? No one knows where that is, but some have driven through it and lived to tell the tale.

Question – Why dirty northern bastards? Answer – Because legend has it that northerners keep coal in the bath. The fact that no one does that any more, and that the practice was never that widespread even back in 't'old days' is immaterial.

Why soft southern bastards? Because legend has it that the southerners are less hardy and play a soft version of football, unlike northern teams which 'get stuck in'. This ignores generations of hatchet men playing for the London clubs, typified by Ron 'Chopper' Harris at Chelsea in the early 1970s.

Before the Industrial Revolution, the north/south divide was not as pronounced. Once it began, the differences accelerated. The need for coal expanded that industry more in the north and Wales than in the south. The move from the countryside into the urban areas created the great northern cities, and the industries they produced made the north dirtier than the south.

When the job losses of the 1980s hit the northern cities, a thousand news reports and documentaries brought out the footage of the General Strike and the Great Depression. This gave us context for what was happening, but also reinforced the stereotypes (at the same time Harry Enfield came out with the character 'Loadsamoney', reinforcing the stereotype of the London wide boy).

We can leave to one side the fact that the south has areas of hardship matching those in the north; that it used to have mining communities, docks and great satanic factories. We can ignore this because we all know that the natural order of things, viewed from the north, is that the south is populated entirely by effete, theatre-going, middle-class softies who probably drink wine and watch foreign films despite them having to be subtitled.

The north, on the other hand, is full of real men who are hardy enough to go through a winter clad only in a cap-sleeved T-shirt with maybe a whippet around the shoulders to keep out the cold.

Mind you, if you look at the south from a southern football fan's viewpoint it is full of sharp, tough Cockney types with a ready wit and a surfeit of diamond geezers. Viewed from the south, the north has a population of barely educated troglodytes who converse in a language comprised mainly of grunts.

The stadium is where the old rivalries, the stereotypes, the identities and the collective memories – some grounded in reality, some not – burn the brightest. Here, in a modern mass-culture, partially homogenised society, the tribes survive and revel in their differences. Anyone seeking to understand this small island off the coast of the Eurasian continent, which has given the world so much, could do worse than to go to Anfield, Old Trafford, Villa Park and White Hart Lane, watch a few games and ask a lot of questions – because some of the answers are there.

In the stadium the differences surface with an exaggerated vengeance. Every stereotype is magnified, and in the religion of football songs, nothing is so sacred that it cannot be sacrificed on the altar of wit. The songs of praise are offered up to the gods on the pitch, while the songs of abuse are usually directed at the opposing tribe with the funny accents from up the road.

It follows, in the logic of football fans, that if you talk different, you *are* different. The alleged moral deficiencies of the north were recognised by Plymouth fans a few seasons ago when they displayed a remarkable concern for that partially hidden blight in our country, domestic violence, with the chant:

Go to the pub – Drink ten pints.
Get fucking plastered – Go back home.
Beat up yer wife – You dirty northern bastards.
Beat up yer wife – You dirty northern bastards.

Mind you, their definition of north is somewhat generous. Bristol City and Bristol Rovers fans, for example, are accused of being 'Dirty northern bastards' by visiting supporters from Devon.

There was a time, not so long ago, when the type of beer drunk before a game could come in handy as a measure of moral worth and degree of masculinity. Sadly, the north has begun to limit its intake of Tetley Bitter, Newcastle Brown and John Smith's. In the future, everyone will drink that great leveller – lager. Lots of it.

Accents, industry, geography, even perceptions of weather all play a role in the banter – everyone thinks Manchester is the wettest place in the world, even though it's only ranked eighth in a list of Britain's rainiest cities. All these perceptions are reflected back through the media in a process that has kept them refreshed. The stereotypes sometimes fade, but then along comes another news event, another documentary, and another comedy regional character that slows the forgetting.

We partly live in another country – the past. In the second decade of the twenty-first century, if you leave to one side accents and a few culinary delights, our lives, north and south, are mostly lived the same way. We accentuate our differences for the purpose of football and/or comedy, but it's mostly pantomime. There's no real deep resentment of each other. I find we mostly like each other, especially if teasing is allowed, preferably with a resounding chorus of 'Soft southern bastards!' Other sports don't have this, but let's face it: golf and lacrosse aren't currently well suited to it.

The stadium with its crowd cover, the residual working-class culture and the acute tribalism of football, all lend themselves to the equivalent of 'He's behind you' calls, but with a lot more swearing. The pantomime is partially based on the same group experience and on which audience it attracts. Like pantomime, football can be a laugh, not to be taken too seriously. However, as we know, everyone in the north is on the dole. Reading fans mistook the Madejski Stadium for a job centre when they taunted visiting Leeds fans with the little ditty, 'You're only here to find a job'. The response of 'We filled your ground for you' met the counter chant: 'We pay your benefits'.

According to some southern fans, there's 'one job in Yorkshire, there's only one job in Yorkshire'. Northerners are at a disadvantage when it comes to the 'one job' chant because there's no riposte. As anyone emerging from Euston or King's Cross for an away game can tell you, there's a McDonald's across the road advertising for a cleaner, and a TGI Friday's nearby wanting a waiter, and so 'Two jobs in London, there's only two jobs in London' simply doesn't work as a football chant. (Middlesbrough had a nice twist on the 'one job' chant with 'One Job on Teesside, there's only one Job on Teesside' in honour of their striker Joseph-Désiré Job, who had six seasons with them in the 2000s.)

The actual rates of unemployment, of course, are more complicated than the chants born of the stereotypes. For example, in early 2014 unemployment in the north-west was running at 7.9 per cent and in London at 8.1 per cent. In the enclave of York, unemployment frequently stands at a quarter below the national average. However, the north-east (10.3 per cent) and Yorkshire/Humberside (8.4 per cent) were both higher than London. If you did do a straight north/south divide you would get higher rates in the north, especially as the south-east as a whole had the lowest rate in the country at 5.3 per cent. These statistics are of no real use to fans from London clubs when visiting Yorkshire because a chant of 'Your unemployment is 0.3 per cent higher than ours' isn't going to get much traction. It is far more fun simply to wave £20 notes and sing 'Stand up if you've got a job'.

Scousers, on the other hand, tend to be accused of having criminal tendencies. This is so well known that even northern fans will happily respond to Liverpool's 'You'll Never Walk Alone' with 'Sign on, with a pen in your hand, and you'll never work again', before demanding to know 'Does the Social know you're here?' Cockneys, which for these purposes means everyone between Stevenage and Southampton, can accompany this inversion of the classic by waving £20 notes at the Liverpool fans. Northerners, especially those from Yorkshire, would not be so foolish as to risk the notes blowing away in the wind and so do not indulge in this practice.

The anti-Scouse songs became fashionable in the 1980s, a decade when Liverpool FC was on a high and Liverpool the city was on a low. Unemployment hit the area very hard and the antics of the local council, led by the sharp-suited, hard-left Socialist Derek 'Degsy' Hatton, who was accused by the former Labour leader Neil Kinnock of wreaking 'grotesque chaos' in the city by 'hiring taxis to scuttle round a city handing out redundancy notices to its own workers', ensured Liverpool was on the news bulletins on a regular basis. Mr Hatton went on to burnish his left-wing credentials by becoming a male model, a PR man, chairman of his son's website company and, currently, a millionaire property developer living in Cyprus. Nice work if you can get it.

The Toxteth riots reinforced the negative image of Merseyside, and fictional figures such as Yosser 'Gizza job' Hughes from Alan Bleasdale's TV series *Boys from the Blackstuff* became synonymous with Scousers.

The loss of life at the Heysel and Hillsborough stadium disasters (in May 1985 and April 1989 respectively) made things immeasurably worse. The death toll was, of course, the biggest tragedy, but both events, in different ways, reinforced the negative stereotypes. Heysel made some people think there was something particularly vicious about the Liverpool fans, even though the behaviour of the hooligan element, leading to the wall collapse, was typical of many followers of the big English clubs at the time. As we know, at the time and subsequently, Hillsborough was blamed on the victims, and the years of searching for justice were met with either indifference or the belief that the Scousers were whinging again.

Liverpool and Everton fans venturing south have been greeted (to the tune of 'Feed the World') by 'Feed the Scousers, let them know it's Christmas time!' If they get bored hearing that, they can also enjoy 'Does the Social know you're here?' and, during the days when Paolo Di Canio played for West Ham, they could head to Upton Park to hear that old favourite, 'We've got Di Canio, you've got our car stereos'. Then there's the cheery – 'Heeeeey eey Scousers! Ooh ah! I wanna know – where's my stereo?'

It's no surprise, therefore, that some Liverpool and Everton fans have been known to turn inwards with the chant 'We're not English – we're Scouse'. There's also the reverse humour song to

17

the tune of The Scaffold's 'Thank U Very Much' – 'Thank you very much for paying our giro, thank you very much, thank you very very very much'. You're welcome.

Tranmere Rovers fans may be from Merseyside, but are keen to point out that they are across the Wirral from the Liverpudlians by singing 'We hate Scousers!', in case anyone mistakes them for a curly haired, moustachioed, tracksuit-wearing, jobless car thief. One of the Tranmere Rovers fans may even be posh. I've never met him or her yet, but you can't rule it out. If so, they may tell you about the Wirral Riviera. The Wirral Riviera? Give over. It doesn't exist. Like the English Riviera, it's a reverie. The Wirral, and the area around Torbay, are perfectly nice places that don't need the Italian word for 'coastline' at the end, but again this appears to be the Tranmere types making damned sure you don't mistake them for a Scouser, or a 'woolly back' from Lancashire. The Scouse accent is possibly the most geographically compressed in the UK. Most of us would be hard pressed to tell a Newcastle accent from a Sunderland one. But move a few miles out of Merseyside and it's instantly recognisable as not Scouse.

As for so much, for that we can blame, or thank, the Industrial Revolution. In the nineteenth century, Liverpool turned into a major international port and attracted a mass influx of workers from north Wales and Ireland. That lies behind what I think is the most distinctive accent in the rich soup of voices within modern Britain.

In the summer of 2011, with the football season over, I was bereft of ideas of how to fill my time, and so I cycled from Land's End up to John O'Groats while waiting for the fixture list to be announced for the following season. It was one of those awful summers when there was neither a World Cup nor a European

Championship. One of the joys of the twelve-day trip was to hear how the regional accents changed as the miles passed, sometimes up to three times a day. We like our accents. They bring a comfortable familiarity. It's a tribal thing, as is so much, but not necessarily negative. For the purposes of football songs, however, it's yet another weapon in the never-ending War of the Banter.

This is why, having heard the Geordie Massive chanting 'Soft southern bastard', in an offensively northern accent, the ranks of the Cockneys will respond, to the tune of 'She'll be coming round the mountain', with 'If you can't talk proper – shut your mouths'. This is not only rude; it's not even proper grammar, innit. This leads to the recent Chelsea chant directed at the hordes from Newcastle – 'Speak fucking English! Why don't you speak fucking English?' The answer to this question is 'Haway an shite bonnie lad we speak Geordie English like'.

So whereas Cockneys might describe the British currency as the 'pahnd', Geordies will say 'poond'. Instead of 'brarn' for brown it's 'broon', and instead of 'tarn' for town it's 'toon'. By the way, Newcastle Brown Ale is not Newkie Brown, as most of us know it, it's simply 'broon', as in having 'a broon down the toon'. That's worth remembering if you walk into the wrong pub at 5 o'clock on a Saturday afternoon after a home game at the Acrylics "R" Us.com stadium and Newcastle have lost.

Geordies can appear very inquisitive to non-Geordie speakers, as so many sentences appear to be a question, with their tendency to inflect up at the end of the sentence? Most of us hear what we think is Geordie when anyone north of Darlington and south of Holy Island opens their mouths. For example, several newspapers have referred to the 'familiar Geordie tones' of Marcus Bentley, aka the voice in the *Big Brother* 'Hoose'. The problem with this? Mr Bentley is from Stockton, which is forty miles south of Newcastle and thus well beyond even a generous definition of Geordiedom.

There was a time when you could almost tell which street someone was from by the first syllable out of their mouths. Before radio, and TV, and the modern transport system, our accents were far stronger than they are today and so very few localised words or expressions would be understood outside of the region. Service in the military brought a few members of the regional tribes together, but until the twentieth century, the numbers serving in the armed forces were relatively small.

These days we recognise some of the Geordie words passed down from TV generation to TV generation. *The Likely Lads* was followed by *When the Boat Comes In*, then came *Auf Wiedersehen Pet* and now *Geordie Bore*. This allows people all over the country to attempt to imitate the accent and come out with something approximating Geordie as it might sound if it was spoken in New Delhi, as opposed to Newcastle. As in most regions, it is softening, but you can still hear it in chants such as 'Toon Army' and songs such as the 'Blaydon Races' – the north-east folksong from 1862, which has passed down the generations partially through the terraces.

Some of the old words can still be heard, i.e. 'bairn' for child, 'marra' for mate, 'wor' for our, but just as the accent is softening, so mass media and transport have 'smoothed' out some of the lesser known terms. It's because of words like 'marra', 'ha'way', 'la', 'bizzies', 'ginnel', 'lakin', 'ey up', 'dibbles' and the rest that some southerners believe Geordies, Scousers, Glaswegians and others to be Neanderthals living in caves and speaking in no known language. I'll have them know that these days the caves have baths and inside toilets, but I'll go there in a moment. In reality, the south has as many accents as the north, but such is the predominance of both 'received pronunciation' and 'Thames Estuary' that they are overlooked.

Our accents, and shrinking dialects, partially define us. Are you sat reading this or sitting reading this? Do you take a bath, a baath, a barf – or indeed a shower? It doesn't matter, it's just interesting. It used to matter more in the 1970s, when we didn't move around the country for work or study as much as now. Then an accent from another part of the country would be instantly noticed, and if it was noticed by the wrong sort of person in the wrong sort of pub, it could spell trouble.

There are two phrases in the English language which to this day cause a chill to run through me. One is 'And if I may say in conclusion', because you know at that point the speech is going to drone on for another twenty minutes. The other is 'You got the time, mate?' By the 1970s, most of us had emerged from our caves and discovered a thing that you fastened to your wrist and which did away with the need for portable sun dials. So the only reason, if you were at an away game, that someone might ask you if you had the time was because they suspected that you supported the away team and wanted to hear you speak.

I'm still not sure which is more difficult: saying whole sentences in a regional accent, or just one word. If you doubt me, try saying 'No' in a broad Cockney or Scouse accent, and then 'I've not got a watch'. Either way, you might get caught out. Remember the film *The Great Escape*? The bit where the Gestapo officer says 'Good luck' in English to the escaped Brit in order to catch him out? Well, apart from the leather coat and the genocidal tendencies of the Nazis, being asked if you had the time at an away game in the 1970s was the football equivalent.

Accents are just one of a thousand sometimes hidden means by which we identify ourselves and others. The north/south identity divide is manifest in many ways. Few supporters in the south will define themselves as southerners, for example, but most northerners will happily be identified as such. Huddersfield, Leeds and Barnsley fans will cheerfully bellow the chantastic 'Yorkshire! Yorkshire!' at the drop of a cloth cap, but I have yet to hear of Watford supporters hymning praise to the great county of Hertfordshire, nor do Gillingham fans break into chants of 'Kent, Kent, Kent!', as far as is known.

I have seen many a White Rose of Yorkshire tattoo adorning the arms of football fans. Indeed, there may even be one on my right shoulder with the word 'Yorkshire' beneath, now faded thirty years after I fell drunk out of a London tattoo parlour with my best mate Paul from Cardiff. There may be, but I can't confirm it. In the event that there is one, it would be there because of the contract you sign, but don't read, before you join the Armed Forces because you're seventeen and unemployed. The small print, hidden under the burly, hairy and tattooed forearm of the recruiting sergeant major, says, 'At some point in your service with the Armed Forces of the United Kingdom, Her Majesty Queen Elizabeth the Second, by the Grace of God, of Great Britain, Ireland and the British Dominions beyond the Seas, Queen, Defender of the Faith etc. requires that you must get at least one tattoo, preferably an ugly one you may regret for the rest of your life. If this tattoo is the name of a girl with whom you later lose touch, and is not the name of the woman you marry when you are older, then you qualify for extra pension.' Always read the small print.

This explains why the only people to have more rubbish

old-fashioned tattoos than football fans are either serving British military personnel or ex-military. Other rubbish tattoos are available, including those arty ones younger types take pride in, not knowing how awful they will look three decades from now. They also don't know that the words on their skin, spelled in a foreign language, which they think mean 'Living each day to the max' actually translate from Mandarin or Arabic into English as 'I am a plonker'.

What I have definitely never seen is the legend 'Surrey' inked across a forearm, although you can't rule it out. However, I do not take this slight cultural difference as evidence of the two nations theory. In 1962, Prime Minister Harold Macmillan made a speech promising to 'prevent two nations developing geographically, a poor north and a rich overcrowded south'. Contrary to the beliefs of professional northerners, snooty southerners, and generations of media types who have made a living out of accentuating the divide through a thousand chippy articles and patronising documentaries, he, and his political successors, were partially successful. I say partially because there *is* a difference between south and north, but too much can be made of it.

I'm arguing that no matter how much we enjoy our sometimes jaundiced view of the other, culturally we are close enough that foreigners visiting these shores may take a long time before they pick up the nuances. There are subtle differences. And even we are not aware of all of them.

As a young and, yes, naïve reporter I was sent to Belfast and ended up filming in a pub that might as well have been called 'The IRA Arms', such was the level of support for the Provos in there. I was working with a cameraman whose name made it obvious, to a local, which side of religious divide he had been born into.

I made the mistake of shouting across the bar to him, 'Hey Billy!' Given that William of Orange was not a popular historical figure in that particular pub, this wasn't the brightest move. The place fell silent, albeit for only a few seconds, before people realised that there was just another idiot English reporter in their midst and not an Armalite rifle-toting member of the UDA. But this is a very specific example in one very specific part of our shared islands, and however instructive it may be, I still maintain that compared to many countries I've visited, on the whole our differences are narrower and matter less. Long may it remain so.

So, look across the picture drawn in broad brush and you see unemployment lower in the south and wages higher, you see longevity lower and poor health higher in the north. There is a political divide: the Labour party remains stronger in the north, the Conservatives stronger in the south, a pattern which became more defined in the late 1980s. Even football stats give an indication of the obvious fact that we have our differences. At the height of the last recession, in a clear reflection of relative job losses, attendances at Premier League stadiums in the north and Midlands fell far more sharply than in the south.

Culturally, however, the modern English are nowhere near as dissimilar as they were a century ago. From Cornwall to Cumbria what unites us is stronger than what divides us. On my two-wheeled journey through England, Wales and Scotland it was apparent that despite our glorious differences, we are also gloriously similar. In 2014 I reinforced my prejudices with a week's holiday in Magaluf. I can report back from the Balearics that no matter if we came from Bangor, Belfast, Blackpool or Brechin, we all showed up in the same cafés for a cooked breakfast, again and again, in time to watch the Premier League game on a big screen.

Social commentators have taken the stats, and the football songs, and the TV programmes, and painted a picture in which the south is prosperous and looks down its nose at the north, which glares back sullenly. Which south, which north? The Cornish don't believe they are swimming in a sea of southern prosperity, nor do the people in Wilmslow think that the economic imbalance has resulted in their town resembling the rougher parts of Whalley Range in Manchester. Tell some people in London's Peckham they are posh snobs and they'll give you both barrels; tell someone in Betty's Cafe Tea Rooms in Harrogate that they speak no known language and they'll grip their bespoke scone tightly before pouring their skinny latte over you.

Only fools and horses truly believe the stereotypes. Dig down and we remain if not glued then culturally woven together. There remains a strong sense of Englishness, and the further north in England you go, 'Britishness'. There's no such word as that (if you spell check it comes out as Brutishness) – but that's another story.

Sure, walk into the wrong pub at the wrong time with the wrong accent and it can all go Pete Tong. However, I'm not going to extrapolate from being told to 'Talk tidy, boy' in Pontypridd, or refused service until I call a pint of bitter a pint of heavy in Dunkeld, that most people behave that way: experience tells us all they don't.

You get some English who go to Wales, have one unfortunate incident with one sour-faced Welsh-speaking miserable bugger, then go home and tell everyone that the Welsh are miserable buggers. People who study logic know a different version of this story, which tells of the man on a train who crosses into Scotland for the first time, sees a field of black sheep and concludes 'Ah, the sheep in Scotland are black'.

And the idea that there might be a sort of physical border between us is a concept few can resist. Which brings us to Wales. It's true that here be dragons and that it is uncharted territory for many English, but some venturing as far as Newport, Cardiff, Swansea or even Wrexham feel they need to remind the home fans that they are in a 'Third world country . . . just a third world country', to the tune of Cuba's finest song – 'Guantanamera'.

As we know, Wales is not a third world country. I used to spend a lot of time in Cardiff and they've got escalators, and the internet, and all sorts; the chant is simply a verbal stick with which to beat your rival, and almost any stick will do. Bristol City and Bristol Rovers fans get a double whammy on the grounds of being only a few miles from the Severn Bridge – 'You're shit, and you're nearly Welsh'. Hey, two for the price of one, don't knock it.

Seemingly embarrassed by this geographic proximity, Bristolians of a certain persuasion have been known to sing, to the tune of 'When the Saints Go Marching In', 'Oh they should have built a wall, not a bridge; they should have built a wall and not a bridge'. Some England fans have taken this up for the rare occasions on which England play Wales.

Of course there is a de facto wall – Offa's Dyke. Offa, King of Mercia, built this barrier *circa* 784 after the Romans had gone home and the Anglo-Saxons began advancing. Three hundred years later, the Welsh weren't having any of that Norman-invasion-1066 non-sense. Unlike the English, who at the first whiff of a croissant and a baguette rolled over and were conquered, the Welsh decided the leek was mightier than the onion. By 1100 they had pushed the Normans out of Gwynedd, Ceredigion and most of Powys. Within a century, in order to celebrate all things Welsh, they inflicted the Eisteddfod on the world.

By the 1400s, Owain Glyndŵr was busy stirring up opposition to the English king, Henry IV, in what is probably the best known period of Welsh resistance. No one knows what became of Owain; he just disappears into history. There are so many caves, churches and hills in Wales in which he is said to be buried that it seems clear to me that he must have been chopped into small pieces and divided up for the good of the future Welsh tourist industry. Anyway, despite his noble sacrifice for Welsh tourism, English repression continued for several centuries even after the Act of Union in 1536, which united the two countries politically. Well into the twentieth century, the Welsh language was still being suppressed.

The Welsh know this history a lot better than the English and so supporters of both the national and club teams give back as good or bad as they get (depending on your view). They need to work on their 'England is full of shit' song and 'We hate England' chant, though, as these are too easy to shrug off. They do better with 'You can stick your Royal Family up your arse', but this works better when addressing teams from the south of England as there is less 'Gawd bless yer, Ma'am' sentiment in the north. Some fans of Wales have been known to chant 'Argentina!' at English supporters. This could be taken as simply a reference to the fact that Argentina beat England in the 1986 World Cup, or it could be a reference to the Falklands War. If the former, then yeah, whatever. But if the latter then they dishonour the memory of the thirty-two Welsh Guards killed aboard the *Sir Galahad* in June 1982 at Bluff Cove.

It's possible that some Welsh fans are not only using anti-English chants to get at the English, they are also proving to themselves just how Welsh they are. Some Welsh speakers have been known to criticise the majority – the non-Welsh-speaking population – for not caring enough about their nationality. What better way to prove them wrong than bellowing 'You can stick your chariot up your arse!' at an England fan? Well, I can think of a lot of better ways, but it seems to work for some.

Some of this is also a way of getting back for being accused of being 'leek-eating sheep shaggers' by the English. Even 'woolly backs' from the northern climes of England sing this on a day out to Newport or Swansea. Normally these 'woolly backs' are themselves accused of having sexual relations with sheep, but they will still join in because, for the day, they are English first, 'woolly backs' second, and therefore far more sophisticated than the Welsh and thus able to accuse them of bestiality before returning north to their pens. I mean houses.

It's hard to tell who Cardiff and Swansea fans pretend to dislike more – the English, or each other. If they're not pretending, then they're really not very clever, and that goes for the rest of the logically challenged in stadiums around the whole country.

At the root of any residual English suspicion of Wales is, I think, language. To this day almost 20 per cent of the population of Wales speaks Welsh. Most English people think of the language of the United Kingdom as English. It comes as a surprise when, as a child, you learn that there are people no more than 100 miles away from any of us who speak a different language, because as children, we think of a different language as a foreign language.

However, in the twenty-first century, the Welsh and English mostly sit down and watch the same TV programmes, go and see the same films, read the same books, and we all eat in Greggs and the local Bangladeshi for our national dishes. Ask someone in Swansea or Scunthorpe if they watched *Strictly* last night and they will both know what you're talking about.

It's a similar story with the Scottish–English relationship. I would argue that the percentage of people in both countries who really do have a problem with each other is higher than in the Wales–England story, and I suspect this reflects the fact that the violence between the two countries is more recent, resulted in more bloodshed, and is commemorated in a highly public manner. And no – I don't mean the Wembley pitch invasion of 1977. By the way, you still owe us a set of cross bars, and kindly stop singing:

We stole your goalposts,
Your lovely goalposts.
We stole your goalposts, and your Wembley pitch too.
You never knew, how much you'd miss them
Till we took your goalposts away.

Just as people in Swansea or Scunthorpe know about *Strictly*, so people in Stirling will also know what you're talking about if you talk about last night's telly. But, always the but, people will answer the *Strictly* question in different accents, or even, a small minority, in a different language. As long as we have these differences they will divide us.

The Scots also know their history better than the English. The Highland clearances, the Battle of Bannockburn, the alliances with France – all are touchstones for Scottish identity. Most Scots know that the song which became the British national anthem once included the verse:

Lord, grant that Marshal Wade,
May by thy mighty aid,
Victory bring.
May he sedition hush,
And like a torrent rush,
Rebellious Scots to crush,
God save the King.

Far fewer English are aware of these lines. Nor are they aware that the word 'Sassenach' is Gaelic for Saxon. We do, however, know that 'Sweaty' is modern Saxon for a Scottish person.

But once we leave the White Cliffs of Dover, or the less White Cliffs of Hull . . . things become simpler.

During the 2004 Euro finals in Portugal, England were doing quite well. I'll say that again, as it is a sentence you can't write often enough, even if you can't write it very often – England were doing quite well. The country was getting behind the team, and the flag of St George had been rescued from the clutches of the far right and could be flown without it meaning you might fancy the odd goose step of an evening. The then prime minister, Tony Blair, was asked if the flag could be flown on government buildings during the tournament. Reflecting that the flag was English, and the Government represents the UK, Mr Blair – he said no.

It was no surprise when, a few days later, with the England–Switzerland game being beamed live back home, and England three–nil up, we heard the following chant:

Are you watching?
Are you watching?
Are you watching, Tony Blair?

I don't know the answer to this question and, like many football fans, for a long time I had mixed feelings about Mr Blair. This was not to do with the Iraq War, or Clause Four, or the repeated inviting of Peter Mandelson into the Cabinet. It was because I was very impressed with his football skills when he played keepie uppie with Kevin Keegan. I'd wager Tony Blair is the only British prime minister in history who could do more than twenty keep ups. As I understand it, Edward Heath could only manage three, and William Pitt the Younger never even tried, despite being only twenty-four when he became prime minister in 1783.

It took some courage from Mr Blair, as he and Keegan were performing in front of the TV news cameras and it could have gone horribly wrong. However, I was very unimpressed when he was reported as claiming that, as a child, he used to go to Newcastle United to see 'Wor Jackie Milburn'.

There were two problems with this. One is that when 'Wor Jackie' retired, Mr Blair was four years old and living in Australia. The other is that he was misquoted and didn't say any such thing, which is a shame as it's a good story. I'm happy to help put the record straight because, as any football fan knows, false claims of support from arriviste fans who only started going to games when prawn sandwiches began to be served are worthy only of derision.

On the other hand, Blair *did* say about the Northern Ireland Good Friday agreement that 'Now is not the time for sound-bites, but I can feel the hand of history on my shoulder' which is unforgivable but not as bad as if he really had claimed to be in the Gallowgate End as a four-year-old.

The 'Are you watching, Tony' chant was born of patriotism, but of the type of patriotism that comes without real malice. Samuel Johnson's famous maxim 'Patriotism is the last refuge of a scoundrel' is often used to suggest he thought it a wholly bad thing. In fact, his friend Boswell said that the great man was referring only to 'false patriotism'. I found this from Johnson's writing:

> It is the quality of patriotism to be jealous and watchful, to observe all secret machinations, and to see publick dangers at a distance. The true lover of his country is ready to communicate his fears, and to sound the alarm, whenever he perceives the approach of mischief. But he sounds no alarm, when there is no enemy; he never terrifies his countrymen till he is terrified himself. The patriotism, therefore, may be justly doubted of him, who professes to be disturbed by incredibilities . . .

I think what he meant to say is 'England fans having a laugh is patriotism, but the racist, overly jingoistic chants are bang out of order and there's really no need to insult the people of a country in which, at away games, we are guests'. Quite right, Samuel.

England fans, indeed large sections of the wider English public, still obsess about the Second World War, and this is reflected in numerous chants. Sung to the tune of 'The Camptown Races', when playing Germany – 'Two World Wars and one World Cup, doo dah doo dah' – is shorthand for the victories in 1918, 1945 and 1966. You might find it jingoistic, but most people sing it without malice towards the Krauts, I mean the Germans. It is just another chant that serves as banter, using shared collective memory, and it is a long way from the songs about Clyde Best, Auschwitz and the Irish Famine (see below).

Put it this way: some of those singing 'Two World Wars' may have shared a drink with a German fan beforehand. The chances of sharing a drink after the game are somewhat less, given that England will probably have lost. On penalties. But before the game they might even have shared a joke, assuming, that is, that they had a sense of humour. The English, I mean.

Only the Neanderthals on each side are really stuck in the past. The rest know that that was then, and this is now, and there really isn't a problem between us – but this is football, so no opportunity will be missed to wind the other up. Speaking of *Homo neanderthalensis*, he is so named because his remains were first found in the Neander Valley in . . . Germany. This may explain why, in the late 1980s, some Neanderthals there caught 'the English disease' and aped their English cousins.

When England play other non-Germanic countries in Europe, the opposition supporters are sometimes reminded, to the tune of 'She'll Be Coming Round the Mountain', that:

If it wasn't for the English, you'd be Krauts
If it wasn't for the English
If it wasn't for the English
Wasn't for the English, you'd be Krauts.

Historians among the England fans might know that this is not strictly true, but anyone attempting 'If it wasn't for the English, and the Scots and Welsh, but mostly the Americans, the Red Army and not forgetting the Canadians, you'd be Krauts' is not going to get very far.

The 'one World Cup' bit in the first chant is also flawed somewhat by the fact that the Germans have won the World Cup, er, four times, and have been runners up four times. It's more a case of 'For you, Englander, ze World Cup is over'.

Our obsession with the Second World War will fade; after all, we've either quite forgotten or quite forgiven the Danes for killing Edmund, king of the East Angles in 869. If they'd killed the king of the North Angles it might have been a different matter, but they didn't, so we forgive them.

However, for now, along with the Falklands War, the two world wars remain central to national consciousness. Hence England fans sing, 'There were ten German bombers in the air, And the RAF from England shot one down, There were nine German bombers the air . . . etc.' (and I mean etc. because it doesn't half go on for a long time), while Scotland fans sing 'There were ten German bombers in the air, And the RAF from Britain shot one down . . .', which is a far more an accurate reflection of the Battle of Britain. Both sets of fans may then break out into the theme from *The Dam Busters* while waggling their arms around in a manner faintly reminiscent of an RAF Lancaster bomber, but often more like a poor parody of an 'Eh? Eh?' Scouser or a 'Little bit waay, little bit whooah' Cockney.

The Second World War was a unifying experience for the UK. In Scotland, apart from a few football-related incidents, both sides of the religious divide pulled together for the national cause, and everywhere the general war effort glued together people who previously might have had very little experience of each other. Football chants notwithstanding, that sense of unity, although frayed, remains today.

For a few years after the war the then predominantly Catholic Celtic fans even put aside their suspicions of the London government's attitude towards Dublin and came up with a song about Hitler's Nazi henchman, Rudolph Hess. Herr Hess had parachuted into Scotland in the deluded belief that he could negotiate a settlement with Britain, despite Hitler knowing nothing about it. He crash landed near Dungavel Castle, South Lanarkshire, was found by a local ploughman, and handed over to the Home Guard. Hence the Celtic song:

A dirty big fat German fell out of the sky one day,
He landed in a corn field not so very far away
And when the farmer's found him he was in an awful
*   mess,*
They asked him what his name was, he replied
*   'Rudolph Hess'.*

So they wined him and they dined him,
And they fed him off the land,
They applied to the Duke of Hamilton,
The affair was simply grand.

Now they asked him what his business was
In Dear Old Glasgow town,
He said 'I've come to Bonnie Scotland
To be on the winning side'.

They then finished off with 'For it's a Grand Ol' Team To Play For, It's A Grand Ol' Team To See . . .' because they did indeed know their history . . .

* * *

No matter how low we can go in our taunting of our southern/ northern/Scottish/English cousins and international neighbours, we can always plumb even further depths for our near neighbours.

A special place in a hellish dictionary is reserved for words for fans from a neighbouring city or county, as we have already seen in the north-east. This is tribalism in microcosm. You really have to look hard for the differences, but it seems to be worth the effort: family arguments are often the most bitter.

Many Liverpool and Manchester United fans display a particularly fierce disdain for each other and each other's cities, which, unless it tips into the sort of abuse that leads to violence, is part and parcel of football rivalry. Social historians trace this back all the way to the Industrial Revolution and the building of the Manchester Ship Canal, which opened in 1894 and brought ships thirty-four miles inland to dock in Salford. Since the 1830s there had been a perfectly good railway line linking the two great cities, capable of transporting goods required for Manchester's factories from Liverpool's port. Then a series of tax rises on imports from the port caused Manchester's business community to think of an alternative, and what better example was there than the recently constructed Suez Canal in Egypt? Or, as a friend from Manchester puts it, 'We thought, well, fuck you then, Liverpool! We'll build our own.'

I'm sure the canal is part of the foundation for the passionate competition between the two clubs, but in recent times I think it has more to do with how one dominated the 1980s, and the other the 1990s and the last decade or so, and that both think they are top dog in the north-west. There's a Man Utd song reflecting this – 'We are the pride of all Europe, the cock of the north. We hate the Scousers, the Cockneys of course (and Leeds!)'

'The cock of the north', eh? In that line we hear their civic pride and a direct line back to the canal; back to which of these great northern cities, both powerhouses in the Industrial Revolution and the most amazing empire the world has seen, was top dog. Before 1894, Liverpool was the economic capital of the north-west. The canal changed that.

In the modern era the two cities compete for tourism, with Manchester attracting more visitors. They also vie for which produces the best musicians and comedians. This is Echo and the Bunnymen v. Joy Division, The Farm v. The Happy Mondays, Steve Coogan v. John Bishop, but more than anything it's Liverpool FC v. Manchester United FC.

And yet. Outside football, this all matters much less. Too much is made of the rivalry between these great cities, and others such as Cardiff and Swansea, or Portsmouth and Southampton. At a football level, yes, there is rock-solid rivalry as each side berates the other for being unemployed, inbred, thieving, cheating, no-mark morons. However, if you're not a football fan, the idea that the neighbouring town is to be denigrated every time it is mentioned is nonsense.

Consider this: does the woman who lives near the Crystal Palace ground but isn't interested in football find it necessary to denigrate the town of Brighton? If someone suggests going down for a day trip on a summer's day, she is unlikely to begin raging, 'I fuckin' hate Brighton. It's full of miserable inbreds, it's full of shit,' and then break into a chant of 'Oh, South London is wonderful'. No, she, like most people, is more likely to say, 'What a good idea, I like it down there.' The same applies to someone similar from, say, Sunderland, if it is suggested they go for a day's shopping at the Metro Centre in Gateshead, or NewcastleGateshead as north-eastern marketing types insist on calling everything within twenty miles of the Tyne these days. The correct response to this modern monstrosity is 'Bah Humbug', or if you are a Newcastle fan – 'Demba Ba Humbug'.

Stuart Maconie, in his excellent book *Pies and Prejudice*, has extrapolated the intense rivalry between two sets of football fans and superimposed it on top of millions of people living in the region. Several other writers have done the same. The argument doesn't hold water. Not only do non football fans not really bother with the rivalry, at least at a serious level, but many football fans don't either. To Manchester City fans, Liverpool FC is just another Premier League rival, a bit like Everton – which doesn't fit the theory of deep dislike between the two cities. So, in context, it's only a minority of people in a city who harbour negative feelings towards an adjacent area, and within that minority, it's only a minority of fans who sing the really abusive stuff.

This is not to underestimate the problem. For example, at Old Trafford, a minority of a 75,811 capacity crowd can still make quite a noise. That minority has updated the old 'In your Liverpool slums' terrace song with several added verses, which do not deserve spelling out, and one which is somewhere near the line:

Your mum's on the beat and your dad's in the nick
You can't find a job 'cos you're too fucking thick
In the Liverpool slums . . .

The original song 'In My Liverpool Home' was written by Pete McGovern and made a hit by the Liverpool folk group The Spinners in 1962, and taken up on The Kop shortly afterwards.

The lyrics include:

In my Liverpool Home
We speak with an accent exceedingly rare,

Meet under a statue exceedingly bare,
And if you want a Cathedral, we've got one to spare
In my Liverpool Home . . .

Liverpool does indeed have two cathedrals, the Catholic one, known as Paddy's Wigwam, and the Anglican one.

Ironically, the song goes on to perpetuate the stereotype of the thieving Scouse scally in the second verse: 'At stealing from lorries I was adept, And under old overcoats each night I slept'.

It then references the city's experience of the Second World War, and its reputation as a tough place, before there's a knowing nod to the Catholic/Protestant divide, which happily is not taken too seriously.

Way back in the forties the world it went mad
Mister Hitler threw at us everything that he had
When the smoke and dust had all cleared from the air
'Thank God,' said the ald fella, 'The Pier Head's still
*   there.'*

. . .

There's a place in dis city were the nits de wear clogs
They've six million kids and ten million dogs
De play tick with hatchets and I'll tell you no lie
A man's a coward if he has more than one eye.

The Green and the Orange have battled for years
They've given us some laughs and they've given us some
*   tears*
But Scousers don't want a heavenly reward
They just want the Green Card to get into Fords.

I remember hearing that on my first visit to Anfield when I was about twelve. I was impressed by the local pride and the acknowledgement of the city's darker side. I learned the words shortly afterwards and my memory of first hearing it is up there with seeing The Kop in full voice during 'You'll Never Walk Alone' on the same day.

That was also the day I discovered that some Liverpool police officers carry really long swagger sticks twice the length of truncheons. I know that because one of them whacked me hard across the legs with one when I didn't move from underneath the stands quickly enough after half time. I didn't complain because he was clearly officer class; only inspectors were issued with the really long ones.

The closest there was to the 'Liverpool Home' folksong that I knew of back home was 'On Ilkley Moor Baht 'at', but the sorry tale of catching your death on the moor due to not wearing a hat, being buried, eaten by worms, which are eaten by ducks, which are eaten by humans and so 'we will 'ave etten thee' never quite spoke to me in the same way. To be honest, it's a bit of a dirge. The only fun bit was adding, after 'On Ilkley Moor Baht 'at', the words 'Where the ducks play football' or 'Where the ducks wear wellies', and even that was never really up there in the pantheon of fun things to do.

To return to 'In My Liverpool Home' (the original), there's widespread recognition that the Scouse accent is exceedingly rare and this is acknowledged along with an extra line when the song is turned back at them – 'You speak with an accent exceedingly rare, you wear a pink tracksuit and have curly hair – in your Liverpool slums'.

If it's Manchester United fans singing this, then back come the cheery Scousers with a reworking of 'Glory, Glory Hallelujah':

The famous Man United went to Rome to see the Pope,
The famous Man United went to Rome to see the Pope,
And this is what he said: Fuck off!
Who the fuck are Man United? etc.

Leeds fans also love to 'hate' Manchester United and for similar footballing reasons as Liverpool, which go back to who won what in the 1960s and 1970s. Leeds had emerged as a powerhouse in English and European football and fancied they could bring down their Lancashire neighbours and their pretensions to footballing royalty.

In Geordie land there are clearly defined borders, but, just as for most of the country, Cockneys are anyone from greater London and a bit more, so Geordies are people from the entire north-east. This does not please denizens of Sunderland, who locally are known as 'Mackems' due to their dialect of the same name but spelt Makkem. Geordies believe that Mackems are called Mackems because you can 'Mackem do anything'.

Middlesbrough? To their Geordie and Mackem neighbours they are known as Smoggies. Where Blackpool has its Golden Mile, so Middlesbrough has its steel-grey miles. Drive past the town on the A19 and you see miles of heavy industry, and towers pumping out smoke and steam. Not too far from them are the housing projects which look as if some bright spark of an architect in the 1960s was inspired to copy from the delights of the industrial eastern Ukrainian city of Donetsk.

We are often defined by our best and worst. Middlesbrough has some fine places, a newish university, a reasonable town centre and that's about it. In other words, it's pretty much like the rest of urban Britain, as in not pretty, but football fans will choose to define it by the worst, because any port in a storm, and any excuse to stick it to the opposition. So Smoggie is a bit harsh, as was the habit, picked up by a minority of visiting Geordies and Mackems, of wearing gas masks to the Riverside Stadium. This went on for several years, eventually accompanied by the donning of white forensic chemical suits to complete the look. By the mid 2000s, the police, having previously said this was not a matter for them, agreed with Sunderland FC and said that they would help enforce the banning of anyone showing up so dressed. Since then the visiting fans have had to settle for singing 'What's it like to see the sun?' and, in fact, by 2010, they were seeing more of that previously strange yellow thing in the sky, as the air quality has improved significantly over the past decade.

Dundee fans refer to Glaswegians as 'Weegies', and some appear to have the same view of them as their counterparts in Manchester have of Liverpool. For special occasions, say when Dundee play Celtic or Rangers, they even use the hubcaps joke via the tune to 'You Are My Sunshine':

You are a weegie
A smelly weegie
You're only happy on Giro day
Your mum's out stealing
Your dad's a dealer
Please don't take my hubcaps away.

It gets worse! Think of the intense rivalry between East Fife (The Fifers) and Cowdenbeath (also known as The Blue Brazil). This is legendary stuff. The degree of antagonism between them is known in football circles as far off as Perth and Pitlochry. (England's equivalent is the rivalry between Northwich Victoria FC and Witton Albion FC. Their stadiums are a mere 500 yards apart and folk as far away as Crewe have heard of their intense competitiveness – happily not put to the test too often due to their being in different leagues.) Cowdenbeath's average gate is around 600; the giants up the road in Methil, home of East Fife, average over 1,300. Given that they are only a few miles apart, they probably all know each other. Some may even have played golf against each other at the splendid course at Lochgelly, just outside Cowdenbeath.

This twist of fate and geography has not given rise to kinship among fans of the two clubs. It has, however, produced a version of the song from the TV series *The Addams Family*, adapted and abridged by the East Fife side of the divide:

> *They're up from near Lochgelly.*
> *They're really fucking smelly.*
> *They've never seen a telly ...*
> *They're the Cowden family.*

A man who has heard this frequently is former Cowdenbeath goalkeeper, miner and legendary cross-bar swinger John Martin. He's a legend partly because he played 702 games in the Scottish leagues (scoring one goal) and just a few years back was still playing despite being in his late forties, but mostly because he was as mad as cheese and all the better for it. He would respond to chants of 'Johnny, Johnny, swing on the bar' by giving a toothless grin and then obliging. We need more goalkeepers like Johnny in the English Premier League.

But back to local rivalry. Twenty years after the miners' strike of 1984, fans from Yorkshire clubs were still taunting Nottingham

Forest and Notts County fans with 'Who let the miners down? – Nottingham – Nottingham'.

On a less political but more anthropological level it would appear, according to modern football songs, that we are all, to a man, woman and child, interbred. There was a time when only fans from the more outlying parts of our great island were accused of congenital defects due to oedipal love. For example, Norwich supporters would regularly hear, to *The Addams Family* theme, 'Your brother shags your mother, Your sister shags your brother, You're the Norwich family'.

However, inbreeding now appears to have swept out of Norfolk and into the whole footballing family. Proof of this comes each Saturday when we regale each other with the charming chorus of 'Your mum's your dad, Your dad's your mum, You're interbred – You X scum'. At this point, insert name of town of said inbreeds before breaking into a chant of 'You've got more thumbs than us; you've got more thumbs than us'. If this is overused, you can always suggest that the good folk of the nearby town have more toes, or indeed ears, than normal people.

Blackburn fans have regaled Burnley, to the tune of 'Yellow Submarine', with 'Burnley fans eat bananas with their feet, bananas with their feet, bananas with their feet', occasionally switching to 'Burnley fans wear their hands on their feet . . .'

Supporters can, on occasion, display a remarkably Christian ability to face up to their own deficiencies before casting aspersions towards the opposition. Just as Jesus said 'first remove the beam out of your own eye, and then you can see clearly to remove the speck out of your brother's eye', so Oldham fans, perhaps in preparation for Sunday school the next day, are known to sing of a Saturday, and with some reverence, 'I'm a bastard,

I'm a bastard, yes I am, but I'd rather be a bastard than a fucking Yorkshireman'.

It's interesting to note here how Jesus uses the word 'brother', thus anticipating the interbred chants by 2,000 years. Perhaps the answer to Blake's great question, 'And did those feet in ancient time, walk upon England's mountains green?', is yes. If so the next question is not so much 'What would Jesus do?' and more 'Who would Jesus support?' To which the answer is – Wakefield Trinity – because he prefers rugby league. Here endeth today's bad joke.

But back to singing. Some of this is in support for your club, but some of it is just part of the day out. You can tell when the team really needs your support as the abusive songs aimed at the opposing fans die away and are replaced by ones aimed at the team.

I've been trying to think of any UK stereotypes which don't translate into football prejudices. I'm still trying. Nope. Can't think of any. In the minds of footballs fans, every passing cliché is grasped, especially as they get closer to a stadium. Norfolk? Straw and tractors. Devon? Cider and farmers, etc.

Most of Britain does it; in fact, most of the world does it. I've never been to a country that doesn't have a region or people about whom the majority makes jokes. When Yugoslavia was a great country of six republics, Tito's communism still couldn't prevent five of the six telling jokes about Moju the idiot yokel from Bosnia. The rough equivalents are the English jokes about the Irish, or the French about the Belgians. In the Arab world, half of the region tells jokes about the 'Gulfies', and in America they tell jokes about Canadians – which is very unfair because it is not the Canadians' fault that they live above a great party to which they are not invited.

We do it locally as well. Recently, I heard radio DJ Robert Elms, who is from North London, joking that he would have to get inoculated in order to take the perilous journey south of the River Thames. Cornwall/Devon, Yorkshire/Lancashire, England/Scotland, next door/both sides – all of 'em – are figures of fun deserving utter contempt and ridicule. The German philosopher Schopenhauer had it about right: 'Each nation mocks the rest and all are justified in doing so'. Mind you, he did go to the trouble of having a footnote saying that in the case of Lancashire there was no justification in mocking Yorkshire.

It is a question of degree; not just how far a song goes, but also how much someone feels it to be offensive. You could argue that the jokes about Scousers reinforce negative stereotypes and so are part of the problem. However, that's not an argument you would win in a debate with football fans, who thoroughly enjoy employing the most useful passing stereotypes in a bid to belittle the opposition. You might find one funny and the other not, one teasing and one abusive, but the terraces retain a strong residue of their male working-class heritage; and working-class humour, like working-class life, is rougher, and what one person might deem abuse, another will regard as teasing.

Here's an example: my brother worked in a supermarket warehouse in t'1990s. At lunch the guys used to banter away the hour. One day they fell to talking about sex. There was a lot of 'you know when . . . ?' So far so laddish. Then one guy said, without it being a joke, 'You know when your missus straps on a dick and . . . ?' In a modern PC office, it would have been the talk of the building, but not to the bloke's face; in the warehouse, though, he endured weeks of people shouting various versions of his story as he passed by.

Another example: I knew a guy who had left his previous employment abroad after allegedly claiming expenses for a lawnmower, despite residing in a flat. I'm sure he didn't; after all, he didn't need one. Anyway, he was a perfectly nice chap, but from a social class where impeccable manners and social decorum counted for a lot. The expenses story filtered through to his new workplace. On his first day he was sitting at a table when a bloke he'd never clapped eyes on showed up behind him and began pushing an imaginary lawnmower up and down an imaginary lawn while making passable imaginary lawnmower noises. This continued until the guy turned round and the room burst out laughing. Workplace bullying or banter?

Whichever it is, it's the way of a certain part of the world, and a certain part of the stadium. In the posh seats people tend not to feel the need to hurl abuse at away fans, nor do they (usually) do this in the family section. These fans are often just as committed to their club as those singing, but they show their support in a different way.

As has been noted, for some, nothing is sacred, and that includes working-class solidarity. We know deep down that most of us are the same, but it matters not. Unemployment, minimum wage, even war, it's all fair game – hence some poor bloke from Nigeria in an ill-fitting fluorescent jacket, who is only doing his job as a football steward, will be reminded that he is on 'Five pound an hour, you're on five pound an hour'. People who sing this are not always avid news consumers and thus not usually up to date with the rate of the minimum wage. I'm not justifying most of this, merely seeking to explain that it is not as aggressive as it might read to some.

The terraces also give crowd cover. Try calling into question Andy Murray's parentage at Wimbledon and it's not only unacceptable to the authorities, but is also unacceptable to your peers, who won't join in, thus leaving you to be the one who is ejected from the premises.

In certain sections of the football stadium there is a feeling that the rules outside don't count. You wouldn't stand in the high street on a Tuesday morning bellowing abuse at people, but somehow, to some, it feels acceptable to do so at football. Happily most fans have limits, even if some are perhaps a little confused. About a decade ago, in a vain attempt to brainwash my son, I took him to a home match. He was about nine years old and I bribed him into making the eight-hour round trip from London by promising it would include as much Coke as he could drink.

In between visits to the toilet, we sat in the family section. In front of us were a father and his four sons. The dad spent seventy minutes screaming obscenities at the ref, the opposing fans and the players. If it had been a night match he would have been howling at the moon. Then his eldest son, perhaps eleven years old, joined in. The man turned, slapped his son up the head, and said, 'I fucking told you not to swear!'

'Quite fucking right,' I thought, apart from the swearing and slapping bit . . . We do need to maintain standards, but we mostly don't do so, or at least some of us don't. I say some, because what is taken as normal football behaviour by many people who never go to matches, is actually abnormal behaviour by the minority.

Many times I've been to a game where a player on a bad run of form has been getting stick from some fans, is substituted, and a few hundred people boo him as he leaves the pitch. The next day I read in the paper that 'the fans booed him from the pitch'. There may have been 30,000 fans present, a few hundred boo, and they become 'the fans'; this is the local journalistic equivalent of interviewing a few student radicals in a faraway land and reporting that the country is on the verge of revolution. It is romantic laziness, also called poor journalism. It's the same with hooliganism; a few do it, and all fans are harmed by it.

The idea that is it socially acceptable to abuse fans because they are, say, Welsh, or English, seems to have surfaced after the Second World War and to have become widespread in the late 1960s. Before this, rivalry between fans of English and Welsh clubs was far more good natured, as it was with most local rivalries. When Portsmouth won the FA Cup in 1939, they paraded it at the Dell, and Southampton fans applauded. Those were more peaceful times – well, apart from the outbreak of the Second World War later that year.

It has not always been the way it is today. Until the post-war period there were far fewer away fans. This was mostly because there was less money about, the train system was not as developed, and many people worked on Saturday mornings. The railways did contribute to football being able to organise itself on a national basis, and they got people to home games, but it would be decades before it was normal for people to travel to away games. However, even if there had been large groups of away supporters to abuse or tease, the culture was different. There was a degree of decorum even in group behaviour.

In 1918 my grandfather came back from four years on the Somme during the First World War with a phrase that became widely used when a swear word was spoken in the company of women. 'Pardon my French' was shorthand for 'I was in the war and I'm still getting used to being back home'. This is not to romanticise life back then. My grandfather was a Methodist lay preacher and a volunteer teacher for the Workers' Educational

Association. Neither pastime lent itself to swearing like a trooper. But he knew that 'industrial language' was generally the norm among men.

The poor and the violent are always among us. From Hogarth's 'Gin Lane' print to Dickens's *Great Expectations*, the chroniclers of our ages have always depicted the harder side of life and there is no reason to think it will change. Nevertheless, in most decades of the twentieth century, large groups of men did not, as standard practice, stand outside pubs near football grounds, mostly drunk, and sing abusive songs before attacking passers-by for possessing an offensive accent. I'm not saying it never happened. The record tells us that the first football banning order came as early as 1314. This wasn't a banning order preventing Johnny Serf from attending Sherwood Forest FC home games, no; this was an order banning football!

Edward II, gawd bless 'im, had become a little concerned at the violence which occurred when rival villages kicked a pig's bladder around the local heath. Why, he feared, next the serfs might want to kick him into touch and that would never do – it could lead to kings and queens of Welsh or even German heritage in charge! I dare say quantities of mead may have been involved in these events.

The past really may not have been so different. Fast forward 571 years to 1885 and we can read of Preston North End fans, or 'howling roughs', attacking both sets of players at a home game. The following year North End were at it again, this time fighting with Queens Park fans in a train station. Preston appear to have been the Millwall of the Victorian/Edwardian era, as in 1905 several fans were put on trial for being 'drunk and disorderly' and a seventy-year-old woman was among the defendants.

According to the Social Issue Research Centre in Oxford, there were occasional incidents of violence in each subsequent decade, but it wasn't until the 1950s that they began to multiply. In the 1955/56 season, Everton and Liverpool fans were involved in damage to trains, and by the 1960s an average of twenty-five hooligan incidents a year were being recorded. The dark side of the game was up and kicking.

What had changed was society. There was now more disposable income to spend on travelling and alcohol. Football exaggerates most things, and as it became more socially acceptable to swear in public, to be drunk in public and to behave as you wanted, so football behaviour reflected societal behaviour in an exaggerated manner. However, I think it's now less violent at football than it has been for decades. The shock of the 1980s led to a flurry of new laws allowing for more arrests, exclusion orders and prosecutions. At the same time, racism began to be taken more seriously and policing became more sophisticated. CCTV and all-seater stadiums have also had a huge influence in changing behaviour. These days, violence is either organised by the psycho firms who, happily, mostly target each other, or things just get out of hand in the way they do every Friday night on national high streets.

Consider the statistics for the 2010/11 season: according to the NCIS Football Unit, in those ten months about 5 million individuals went to see a professional football match. In the same period there were 3,089 football-related arrests. Maths is a foreign language to me so I can't do the percentage, but I know it's pretty low. Also, some time in the last decade, football hooliganism just went out of fashion. There are so many other things to do with your time these days. I'm convinced it could make a return, though, as bad as ever, given the wrong circumstances.

You don't actually 'hate Cockneys', you don't really 'hate Manchester', you don't 'hate Portsmouth' and if you don't understand that the opposing fans are actually you – just with a different accent and a different pie – then you're thick. Sorry, did I say that out loud? For the rest of us, yes, we can wind each other up, we might even have a genuine dislike for jellied eels, or deep-fried Mars bars, or whippets, but we don't hate each other, and the professing of 'We hate Liverpool, too (and Leicester)' is neither meant nor supposed to be believed.

The stand-up comedian Michael McIntyre tells a joke about being in a Yorkshire video rental shop and, to ensure he is understood, asks if they have Clint Eastwood's 'T'Good t'Bad and t'Ugly'. No one is supposed to believe that that is what a Yorkshire person would say, and in the stadium no one expects the opposition fans to be offended when they are informed of their various mental and ethical deficiencies at great length and volume.

There are those who feel that every gentle dig, every joke, is an attack on 'the other', feeding into the stereotypes which feed into racism, oppression and violence. There is a sliver of truth in that, but only a sliver. This argument is usually made by people who don't joke, who don't have a laugh with friends who are different, and who can't tell the difference between a joke or chant which is intended as fun, and something vicious. They are usually academics and/or deeply political and they live in their academic and deeply political worlds. They see the world through a prism of human rights and political correctness. The rest of us live with each other, each of us belonging usually to several tribes at the same time, and mostly we get on fine.

Intellectuals tend to see tribalism as a primordial force that will eventually wither on the vine of flourishing universalism and globalism. They imagine all the people living in harmony. No, wait, that's John Lennon. They imagine a world where the colour of a man's skin is of no more significance than the colour of his eyes. No, hang on, that was Haile Selassie, as quoted in one of Bob Marley's best songs – 'War'. I'll give it another shot; they imagine a world where northerners will no longer insist that fish and chips are better 'oop' north than down south. And there is the flaw in their argument.

Basically human beings *want* the fish and chips to be better where they are. It gives them a sense of belonging and that gives a sense of security, which is what we've always wanted. It gives us an anchor in what are often turbulent lives. So Grimsby fans will attach themselves to the cliché that they are all trawlermen and sing 'Swing low – sweet halibut', while Wrexham fans will sing, instead of 'Bread of Heaven', 'Wrexham Lager, Wrexham Lager, feed me till I want no more (want no more), Feed me till I want no more'. Thus they localise what is a national song. Plymouth fans just stick to their region, chanting 'Ciderrr, Ciderrr, Ciderrr' over and over again, quite possibly having drunk several gallons of the stuff before the match.

There really is a beer called Wrexham Lager, which the company says is Britain's oldest lager brew, a claim based on the brewery being founded by German immigrants in 1882 to make up for having to drink that dark room-temperature stuff in which the weird island race of Britons indulged. Apparently there is evidence of Wrexham Lager being drunk by the British soldiers at the siege of Khartoum in 1884–5. If this is true, it might go some way to explaining why General Gordon came a cropper. It was also served on the *Titanic*. Now it's served in Wrexham, which has a football team in the Blue Square Bet Premier Conference, despite it once having been a top-four division full-time professional club. There's a pattern emerging here.

Anyway, this fine drink is much beloved in the town, and beyond, and gives Wrexham fans a reason to celebrate local beer, local pride, and the sense of difference so crucial to having a well-developed sense of superiority and dislike towards visiting fans. If Eccles FC was in the Premier League, I'm sure there would be a song extolling the superiority of Eccles cakes to all other similar pastries. The trick is to keep the sense of difference at the level of fish and chips, beer, cakes and pies. Never forget the pies. I'm confident that fish and chips are better up north, but I wouldn't go to war over it.

At another level, that of war, I know Israelis and Palestinians who are friends and who socialise with each other. They will, however, still argue passionately about whose hummus is better. If they can resolve their differences, on a day-to-day human, hummus, non-political level, so can we.

One of the great things about us is our differences. For an example of how boring we would be if we were all the same, watch an episode of *Star Trek – The Next Generation* to see a vision of a banter-free future. You know when Captain Jean-Luc Picard runs out of the bridge with an away team, en route to beaming down somewhere? Well, the Starship *Enterprise* is massive. It must take ages to get down to the transporter. Imagine being stuck in a lift with that lot. Mind you, I always had a soft spot for that Lieutenant Deanna Troi who could read people's minds. Half-human, half-Betazoid. I've always liked that in a woman.

Captain Kirk was much more fun in the original series, and he snogged Lieutenant Uhura in the first multi-racial kiss on American TV. However, it was *The Next Generation* which gave sci-fi one of its greatest lines about what it is to be human. Picard (a Huddersfield Town fan) had taken some sparkling grains of sand up to the *Enterprise* to analyse them, as you do. The sand quickly reversed the role, took over the ship and then asked the crew: 'Ugly giant bags of mostly water – why are you trying to hurt us?'

Where were we? Oh yes, the point being, some of us might sing something at a game on a Saturday about a nearby town, then go to work on Monday and joke about it with a workmate who was in the opposite end. There are thousands of people who are exceptions to this and who are vile, but there are hundreds of thousands of the rest of us who take exception to these ugly giant bags of mostly water.

They've always been with us and we've been writing about them from the riots at Roman chariot races to the East End thugs in *Great Expectations*. What football has done is give cover and a false rationale to the thugs. They can even convince themselves that they are the righteous ones, defending the honour of their team, region, or country. Some sociologists tell us the hooligans are part of the British underclass. That's not true in my experience, and unless they are successful criminals, few in the real underclass can afford £100 for an away day at football. I know company directors and estate agents who are or have been hooligans, some of whom are smart enough to have made their way in life, but stupid enough not to be able to control their enjoyment of violence.

There are indeed men who go to grounds and spend most of their time facing not the pitch, but the direction of the opposition's fans. They gesticulate in an odd simian manner, palms out, legs akimbo, mouths open. Put a pond between the two sets of fans who do this and it would be like a re-enactment of the opening scene from *2001: A Space Odyssey*. They pay £30 to stand and look at a group of people thirty to forty yards away. I suppose if it was a north/south game they might be trying to spot signs of cultural differences, or listening to hear if the opposition were speaking in any known language. However, if it's a local derby, they could instead just go to the shopping centre the following day and look at everyone for free. The rest of us spend money to watch the game.

Where it gets really serious is when the organised firms get involved, albeit usually with each other. Then there is the dwindling minority who go in for racist chanting, and, sadly, the non-dwindling section of Celtic and Rangers fans who really, really, seem to care who is a Catholic and who is a Protestant. In England, hurling abuse at your fellow countrymen because they are northern, or southern, or whatever, is done without it touching the raw nerves of recent history. As discussed, there are old rivalries, but in Scotland it gets more serious.

At Celtic v. Rangers games there are those on one side who want to be 'up to our knees in Fenian blood', and those on the other celebrating the IRA. In the 1970s you could occasionally hear similar chants on the terraces in England, but I doubt whether many of those then indulging in 'UDA all the way – fuck the Pope and the IRA' songs were engaged in a religious struggle, whereas at Celtic and Rangers you get the impression that they really feel themselves to be warriors in a sectarian war. Here is a sub-tribe within a sub-tribe within a tribe, by which I mean, in order, those prepared to bring sectarian politics to the game; football fans; and to the Scottish.

A good example is the Bobby Sands song. Sands was the first of the IRA hunger strikers to die. Regardless of what you think of his gesture, singing, 'Do you want a chicken supper, Bobby Sands?' at fans who are Catholic is hardly likely to bring the two sides closer together. The 'Fenian Blood' song referred to above originates in the 1920s and is called 'The Billy Boys'. It celebrates a Glasgow Protestant gang led by Billy Fullerton, which used to fight with Catholic gangs. Those who would sing it have their opposite numbers among the Celtic fans who, when not banging on about the IRA, may celebrate the Ibrox Disaster or break into a version of 'The Merry Ploughboy', with lyrics changed to niceties such as 'We're all off to Dublin in the Green – fuck the Queen'.

The Ibrox Disaster of 1971 resulted in sixty-six Rangers fans being killed in a crush on the stairs coming out of the ground. Some Celtic fans have been heard singing about 'Huns lying on the stairs'. Huns refers to the Protestant Hanoverian royal dynasty and the fact that the British Royal Family are descended from Germans. Of course, there are many fans of both clubs who don't get involved in this primitive nonsense, but for sheer numbers singing offensive songs, these two are top of the pile, beating only the troglodyte sections of The Kop, the Stretford End and the Shed. (And Leicester.)

I don't want to go on about this too much, partly because I don't want to give the many mainly decent fans in Glasgow a bad name, and partly because it remains an ambition to go and see a Celtic v. Rangers match. Or Rangers v. Celtic. I'm not taking sides here. It is likely that most of those indulging in the sectarian hate chants would not follow through on their blood-curdling threats, and that they feel it's simply part of supporting their club; but to an outsider the divide is wider than anything else in British football. Too wide.

Before we move on, a brief history of the background of this divide and then a précis of a court case in Kilmarnock which makes fascinating reading. It concerns a match at Kilmarnock involving

Rangers, which was attended by 10,150 people, 6,489 of whom were Rangers supporters.

First the history: the Irish were coming to Scotland as seasonal agricultural labourers long before the famine of the 1840s, which is estimated to have killed up to one million people. However, during and after the famine of 1846–7, the numbers swelled and people began to stay on, particularly in the west of Scotland. The 1851 census has 18 per cent of people in Glasgow being Irish-born, whereas across to the east in Edinburgh the figure was 6.5 per cent. Almost all the immigrants were Catholic in what, since the Reformation, had been a staunchly Protestant country. Tensions soon arose, especially in working-class districts, as there was competition for unskilled jobs.

Fast forward a few decades and by the 1880s, substantial numbers of Irish Protestants were also coming over. There were pockets of what were perceived to be Catholic or Protestant neighbourhoods, although the divisions were never as pronounced as they were in Belfast. At the same time, the first professional football clubs were being formed. Many of them grew out of church teams and, in Scotland, Celtic FC grew out of the Catholic community in Glasgow. But that was at a time when people identified themselves more by their religion than they do now. The Scots now attend church, on a regular basis, more than the English do (about 10 per cent compared to 5.5 per cent), but let's face it, with percentages like that, religion does not play a big part in most of our lives.

And yet, in football, it still seems to matter to some. To twenty-year-old William Walls in 2009, it mattered so much he was convicted of various heinous offences in a court case which is also a sorry tale from the terraces. Mr Walls, a Rangers fan, appealed against his conviction and it fell to Lord Carloway to assess the evidence. According to the court records, Mr Walls had been accused of 'at Rugby park [. . .] Kilmarnock you [. . .] did conduct yourself in a disorderly manner, shout, swear, sing sectarian songs, shout remarks of a religious and racial nature [. . .]'. Several people gave evidence that he had been heard to suggest that someone should have sexual relations with the Pope, was shouting 'Fenian bastards', and singing 'the famine song'. A police superintendent said this referred to the Irish Famine and to people of Irish descent, who lived in the west of Scotland. The song carries the refrain 'the famine's over, why don't you go home'. Rangers FC have tried to curb it by threatening to ban fans who join in. Celtic have similar policies for some of the songs their fans sing. It's worth noting that both clubs have supporters' groups trying to rid the terraces of sectarian bigotry.

Mr Walls turned up for his first hearing wearing a Rangers FC replica shirt.

His legal team made a fascinating defence. Even if he had been singing the famine song, which was denied, the song 'did not contain racist elements [. . .] the refrain "the famine is over, why don't you go home" was not racist. It was just an expression of political opinion permitted by the general right of freedom of speech [. . .] It was no more racist than some of the lines in "Flower of Scotland", which bid King Edward to return to England to think again [. . .]'.

'Fenians', it was said, was a reference to the Fenian Brotherhood, a political society, set up originally in America in the 1850s, to bring about the independence of Ireland. His defence also argued that 'an exchange of abuse between supporters was part and parcel of going to a game. Shouting and swearing was commonplace.'

In the original judgement the court had 'no doubt that the conduct of the appellant did amount to a breach of the peace, even in the context of a football match where at least shouting and singing, or hearing shouting and singing, are undoubtedly part of the match experience expected by all attending the stadium [. . .] However, presence inside a football stadium does not give a spectator a free hand to behave as he pleases.' It then used legal jargon to say 'Fenian Brotherhood? America? Political? Get outa here . . .' and ruled that the defendant's behaviour was, in fact and in law, religious bigotry and that calling for 'people native to Scotland to leave the country because of their racial origins' was racist.

Lord Carloway agreed and the appeal was refused. Mr Walls's sentence of two years' probation was upheld. He was also banned for life from Ibrox by Rangers FC. His Lordship also stated that 'there are many spectators at football matches who actually want to watch the game rather than spend their time abusing the opposition support'. For his wisdom, we may thank the Lord. Obvious though this may be to most fans, it's a fact not always recognised by those who equate football supporters with hooligans.

* * *

Now, here's the thing, as we don't say in this country. As a Yorkshireman I have absolutely no problem with the gross insult that being a bastard is better than being a Yorkshireman. Why? Two reasons: firstly, any Yorkshire man or woman knows that the chant is borne of a deep sense of inferiority on the part of those singing it. Secondly, it has also been known for some time by sociologists, historians, weather forecasters, and gastronomes that the only good thing coming out of Lancashire is the M62. More seriously, the chant counts as banter and is usually taken as such.

Ah, banter – the cover for many a chant from both previous and current times which is actually grossly offensive, indeed, on occasion, vile. However, there is an acceptable level of banter and most of us know where to draw the line. Questioning whether a certain player has a genuine birth certificate falls one side of most supporters' line; hoping that a player's children contract a terminal illness falls a long way over the other.

I've done hundreds of interviews for this book, and in almost every one, the word banter has come up. Banter is social interaction. There are no set rules telling us what is and isn't acceptable; we just feel our way towards the invisible lines. Where you could use the argument, and get agreement, is if you attach it to the issue of racism.

We've come a long, long way since the 1970s, when several thousand men thought it was acceptable to simultaneously bellow at the wonderfully talented West Ham legend Clyde Best 'Zigga Zagga Zigger – Clyde Best is a N****r!' Albert Einstein may have had people like this in mind when he said: 'Only two things are infinite, the universe and human stupidity, and I'm not sure about the former.'

By the way, there's an Albert Einstein Academy of Football in California. Sadly this is an American football academy where sissies wear lots of padding, chase an egg around the pitch, and then run into each other. They wouldn't last the first five minutes of a Widnes v. Pontefract match. It's not a 'Soccer' academy as it should be. Einstein would surely have been a fan of the relatively superior game. Theoretically.

Anyway, it is now inconceivable that a black player at the top level in the UK would be subjected to the type of abuse Clyde Best endured, especially from so large a number of people. We have been educated, and have educated ourselves, through a long, painful period. There are still racists, but the difference is that there are now enough of the rest of us to make it socially unacceptable to use the N word even at that bastion of defiance to the PC world – the football stadium. And if a twelve-year-old doesn't hear thousands of people chanting it, then he or she is more likely to think it unacceptable to do so. People do still use the term, but not in groups of three thousand.

Racism is one of those examples that prove how, if the law changes, then culture can change. The Race Relations Act became law in 1976, in which the police were given extra powers to prevent incitement to racial hatred. I would include the Clyde Best chant in that category. Since 1976, then, through a mixture of law and education, and growing up as a nation, racism on the terraces has been diluted.

There have been black Brits for hundreds of years, but only in large numbers since the 1950s. It has taken those decades for the majority of the population to adjust to a new reality. It hasn't been easy. However, in this case, familiarity has not bred contempt. Quite the opposite. And as it has become the norm to live in a multi-ethnic urban society, levels of racism appear to have decreased. I'm not arguing it's perfect, I'm simply saying it's not what it was, but it is a national work in progress. Chuck a banana at a black player now and there's a reasonable chance that if the CCTV cameras don't pick you out, one of your own supporters will have a word in the ear of a steward or a policeman.

After the N word became recognised for what it is, there was still a way to go. Well into the 1990s you could still hear chants such as 'town full of Pa*is' or 'I'd rather be a Pa*i than a Scouse'. That too has mostly gone, at least from the stadiums.

The reason that one chant is banter and another pure racism lies in the context. It may not be very nice, as a Norwich or Ipswich fan, to be accused of being inbred, but those subjected to the taunt are not inbred, and they don't suffer any further indignity once they leave the ground. Nor, I would hazard, do they really care what those they regard as Cockney Muppets or Northern Monkeys think of them. But introduce race in a negative manner and you change the context. Those prepared to use such language are not joking, because they know how offensive they are being.

This is tricky territory. Not all chants connected to race are necessarily racist. A few years back, Jason Lee of Nottingham Forest was a player who both was black and had an alarmingly flamboyant hairstyle. To the tune of the old American spiritual song 'He's Got the Whole World in His Hands', he would be taunted with 'He's got a pineapple on his head'. Racist? Well, he wore his hair in a way white men would struggle to achieve, and the pineapple is vaguely tropical, but really the chant was less to do with his race, and more to do with him looking as if he had a pineapple on his head. Many players, of whatever race, are given grief if they depart from 'a side parting, a bit off the top and neaten it at the back please, not too short'. To some the pineapple chant is racist, to others it is 'just' acceptable football terrace behaviour, somewhere along the banter-to-abuse spectrum.

Older fans will remember the Newcastle song aimed at Peter Reid, who has a footballing brain to die for, a well lived-in face, and was guilty of being the manager at Sunderland for seven years. For this heinous crime the Toon Army sentenced him to seven years of the song 'Oh Peter Reid – he's got a monkey's heed'. Now, that's really not very nice, especially if you are Peter Reid. But I doubt he gave a monkey's heed about it.

Back to racism; there are degrees of it. 'Town full of curry' aimed at somewhere like Blackburn is clearly racist. Even more racist is 'Your town smells of curry'. Why? You know why. It's not funny. It's really, really not funny, and there's no way of arguing that it is anything but offensive. That's the difference between a racist chant, an abusive chant and one that is borderline teasing. I'd argue that the one below, aimed at our friends in Hartlepool, is banter/teasing.

Hartlepool fans are called 'monkey hangers'. Unlike a racist chant, this one is up for debate about whether it's offensive or whether it's funny, or, of course, whether it's both, or neither. In footballing circles, Hartlepool is famous as being the place where a French shipwreck during the Napoleonic wars threw up a poor bedraggled monkey wearing a French uniform, thought to be for the amusement of the crew. Our simian friend was taken to be a French spy by local people and dragged off to the authorities. After a fair trial, in which the prosecution pointed out that the defendant couldn't speak English, the poor thing was hanged by the neck until dead.

This explains both the 'monkey hangers' moniker, and two other things. Firstly, the Hartlepool FC song:

Old folks, young folks, everyone of each,
Come and see the Frenchy has landed on the beach.
He's got long arms, a great long tail, he's covered all
    in hair,
We think he's a spy – so we'll hang him in the square.

It also explains how, in 2002, Stuart Drummond, the then Hartlepool FC mascot, 'H'Angus', stood as Mayor for Hartlepool, campaigned wearing a monkey suit, promised everyone free bananas, and was duly elected. Three times in a row.

So far, so funny, unless you disagree and think the whole thing distasteful and indeed disrespectful to monkeys and intend getting a posthumous pardon for the French spy, I mean the monkey. Old habits die hard and the English are still sticking it to the French whenever they can. To call the French 'Frogs' is surely xenophobic, but is it possible to be xenophobic and funny? You can judge from this Leicester City chant when Arsène Wenger's French-dominated side took to the pitch. To the tune of the Baha Men's 'Who Let the Dogs Out', they came out with 'Who let the Frogs out – Who? Who? Who? Who?'

Songs often play on stereotypes. They may not be fair but that does not necessarily mean they are malicious. A good example is the song for China's Sun Jihai when he was at Manchester City, which was to the tune of 'She'll Be Coming Round the Mountain':

Singing aye aye yippy Sun Jihai,
Aye aye yippy Sun Jihai,
Singing aye aye yippy,
His dad's got a chippy,
Singing aye aye yippy Sun Jihai.

To some people, any song that refers to race is racist, to others it might be fun, and/or an acknowledgement of the undeniable – we are different even if we are the same. This is one of the UK's many 'culture wars'. Journalists covering the USA regularly write about the culture wars there; we appear to be less aware that we are fighting very similar battles here.

The fans really liked Sun Jihai (or Jihai Sun, as he preferred to be called, even though it was too late to turn it round by the time he signed for City from Crystal Palace in 2002). When he arrived in England in 1998, along with Fan Zhiyi, they became the first Chinese players to play professional football in the English leagues. Sun went on to become the first Chinese player to score in the Premier League, with a goal against Birmingham City in October 2002. A header no less. As far as is known, Sun Jihai senior did not have a fish and chip shop in Manchester, nor in Manchuria. The chant is therefore based on the old stereotype about what Chinese people in the UK do. As with many stereotypes, there is a degree of truth behind it – and for that we can thank the washing machine.

The first report I can find of a Chinese laundry opening in the UK is in 1877, in the *York Herald*, when readers were told that London's West Kensington district was about to be graced with one. Riots ensued amid fears of an invasion of the 'Yellow Peril' – this was not helped by Sax Rohmer's novels about Dr Fu Manchu and his fiendish plots in the Docklands area of London. The lead character's signature characteristics ranged from him being an evil genius to being an evil cunning genius with an evil moustache. In all, thirteen Fu Manchu novels came out but they were all more or less the same book with different titles – a bit like Sir Alex Ferguson's autobiographies.

By the 1930s there were over 500 such laundries. Then some damned fool invented a washing machine, which could be powered by electricity and, more importantly, mass produced to make it affordable. My grandmother couldn't be doing with these new-fangled things and carried on with her tub and mangle into the early 1980s. Mind you, she did have a proper bath, with taps and everything. I was proper posh because I had two baths a week. One I had at home in a tin bath in front of a three-bar electric fire, parked reassuringly close to the water, and then a second, at my grandmother's. Happily, at about the age of nine I moved into a house with a bath that was connected to hot water. Luxury. Sorry to come over all Four Yorkshiremen for a moment, but this was a real step up from the maxim of my beloved late stepfather, Ronald McDonald (no, really), which was that when he was a boy, he had a bath once a month whether he needed it or not.

Anyway, many Chinese moved into another area of self employment in which they could compete with the majority population: the catering industry. This explains why, by the 1970s, it was highly likely that the local chippy down the end of your street was Chinese owned, as was almost certainly the Golden Dragon restaurant in the town centre. Mind you, I once went to an Indian restaurant in Portsmouth owned and operated by Italians. But only once.

The chippy gave us what we now know as one of the great British traditional dishes: chips and curry sauce with scraps. The restaurants made us realise that Vesta Chow Mein in a packet was not actually Chinese food but British cardboard, only to be eaten after several units of alcohol and if you couldn't find a kebab stall open near the bus station.

Back to Sun Jihai – and this from the Manchester City FC website – '[. . .] the recipient of one of the last decade's funniest City terrace chants – which, whilst possibly not passing a political correctness or diversity test, nevertheless brought smiles to those who heard it, including the player himself.' Indeed. He went back to China in 2009 but made an emotional return to Manchester in 2011, where he was introduced to the fans in a pre-match ceremony. The warmth with which he was greeted almost overwhelmed him, and the bond between player and fans was clear to see.

In an interview with MCFC TV, he spoke movingly about how he loved the fans and loved to hear them singing his name. With a slight smile he invited any Man City fan visiting China to get in touch and said he would personally take them to a Chinese restaurant, where they could learn more about his national cuisine. I assume chips won't be on the menu.

The stereotyping of Sun Jihai, and even the songs about Korean footballers eating dogs, are a long way from the pure racism of the 1970s and the illiberal use of the N word. However, when it comes to anti-Semitism something strange happens.

Which bring us to the word Yids.

Why put an asterisk for the N word, and the P word, but write Yids in full? Is it not as bad as the others? The answer is yes, but it is written in full simply because many people are not even aware it's an issue, and don't know the word. What is strange is that even though the type of person who used to bellow the N word at games now know they can't get away with it, they do still use the Y word.

Some, and it's important to say only some, Spurs fans call themselves Yids. Why? Because Tottenham does indeed have a larger minority of Jewish fans than do most clubs, and many opposition supporters are aware of this. Are most Tottenham fans Jewish? No, but because of history, anti-Semites called them all Yids, and just as some black Americans appropriated the N word, so some Tottenham fans say they have appropriated the Y word. Many Tottenham fans join in the chant 'Yiddos', and the flag of Israel can very occasionally be seen on the terraces at White Hart Lane.

The association of Spurs with Jews began before the Second World War, but it only became a terrace issue and material for songs in the 1980s. By the following decade, anyone walking up Tottenham High Road on a match day would be greeted by a massive flag hanging out of a pub window near the ground bearing the legend 'Yid Army!', often accompanied, after several pints, by the chant 'Yid Army!' Some Jewish Spurs fans join in this chant; some are deeply offended by it. In 2012, the FA tried to ban the chant, with the obvious result being that the ban was totally ignored. At the next game one of the first chants was 'We're Tottenham Hotspurs – we sing what we want', followed by 'Yid Army!'

Given that some Jews join in the chant, it would make a fascinating legal case if they were arrested and went to trial charged with anti-Semitism. Less legally complex would be the arrest of West Ham fans who turn up at White Hart Lane and sing 'Big nose. You've got a fucking big nose'. You wouldn't need several years of legal training to argue how offensive and anti-Semitic that chant is.

If anyone thinks there are no Jews who would join in the Yid Army chant, then they don't know football fans. I will never forget going to Stamford Bridge with a Jewish Chelsea fan who is a season ticket holder in the Matthew Harding stand. It was the week before the Spurs–Chelsea game and thousands were singing: 'We'll be running round White Hart Lane with our willies hanging out, singing I've got a foreskin, have you?' My Jewish friend joined in. This is one of many examples of how weird supporting a team can be. I didn't see any women joining in this particular chant. That would have been even weirder, but only just. Bring on Sigmund Freud, but only if you're two down in the second half.

When Spurs fans chant 'Yid Army' it may or it may not be anti-Semitic; but it certainly is if an opposing fan does it. Even so, it's on a different level entirely to one of the most vile chants ever to be dredged from among the worst elements produced by our country. In 1981 Spurs released a record (as we called them in those days) called 'Ossie's Dream (Spurs Are on Their Way to Wembley)'. It was full on Chas and Dave, 'knees up, knees up, gawd bless yer sir' stuff and it is still to be heard at White Hart Lane to this day.

Alas, visiting fans from Leeds, Chelsea, West Ham, and possibly other clubs, have reworked this into something worse than the anthem of the Nazi Party, 'The Horst Wessel Song' – 'Spurs are on their way to Auschwitz, Hitler's gonna gas 'em again – the Yids from White Hart Lane'. The song ends with a hissing sound to invoke an image of the chambers, accompanied by the wiggling of fingers to represent the gas coming down.

I've heard this several times. The only solace I can take from it is that, of perhaps 3,000 away fans, only about 300 joined in, and of those, only some have the wit to truly understand what they are doing. Those who do are the ones who might even perpetrate such crimes, given the wrong circumstances, and those who don't know what they are singing are the sheep that would be caught up in the madness. They are also the ones who sing, with Adolf Hitler in mind, this little gem of ordure: 'He's coming for you, He's coming for you. We won't say his name, but he's coming for you.'

The association of Tottenham Hotspurs with Jews goes back to the early twentieth century, but is exaggerated and based on two false premises, including one that that religious Jews were allowed to take trams on the Sabbath to get to games. Since roughly the 1950s, the largest population of British Jews live in North London. Significant numbers of the most obviously Jewish community, the Ultra-Orthodox, are in Stamford Hill, which is near White Hart Lane. So the idea has grown up that when the first Jewish immigrants began arriving in the late eighteenth century, they went on to choose Tottenham because of its geography.

There are two flaws in this argument. First, the 'black hatters', as the Ultra-Orthodox are sometimes called, tend not to go to football matches anywhere, not even in Israel. You can see the odd kippah at White Hart Lane but very few. Pork pies? Yes. Kippahs? Not so much. Second, in the first few decades of the twentieth century, the majority of Britain's Jews lived not in north London but closer to the East End. The nearest club was West Ham: the combustion engine buses went east, but the electric tram lines ran north towards Tottenham.

It has been argued, in the august pages of the *Wall Street Journal* no less, as well as elsewhere, that there was a rabbinical decree forbidding Jews to travel on buses on the Sabbath, but permitting them to use trams, as these did not transgress the biblical injunction against making fire on the holy day. This is nonsense, as any rabbi with a doctorate in Torah studies and a GSCE in physics could tell you. The ban on driving on the Sabbath comes from the book of Exodus, the idea being that creating fire is work and the Sabbath is a day for rest and study. Taking a bus powered by an internal combustion engine transgresses the law. What? And taking an electric tram doesn't?

I've read Exodus, chapter 35, verse 3, and the commentary on it – I expect you have, too – and I've yet to see the bit where it says 'I've told you no making fire – unless you're going to see my chosen team on a tram'.

Oh, there's another myth right there – the idea that Tottenham is God's chosen team. It is clear to me that God's chosen team resides in a large English northern city but is currently condemned to wander in the wilderness, also known as The Championship, possibly for forty years, for some transgression in the past – perhaps for getting relegated.

The forty years thing is to allow the current generation to die out and only the new generation to see the Promised Land, which, as you can see, has the same initials as – the Premier League. Or, to quote God at length: 'So the Lord's anger burned against Israel, and He made them wander in the wilderness forty years, until the entire generation of those who had done evil in the sight of the Lord was destroyed.'

Serious estimates more recently put the Jewish population at Spurs games at 5 per cent. Arsenal are thought to attract similar percentages. Tottenham fans, including Jews who sing 'Yid Army', argue that they have appropriated the word and turned it back on the anti-Semites. It is argued that the use of the term is the same as blacks using the N word. I'll take that up to a point from Jewish Spurs fans, but not from the other 95 per cent. I agree with David Baddiel, who says non Jews using the word in this context are like white men in predominantly black neighbourhoods calling themselves 'N*****s'.

However, Stephen Pollard, editor of the *Jewish Chronicle*, makes a strong argument in defence of the Yid word on the terraces on the grounds of humour and turning the word back on the Neanderthals. I rang him for a five-minute argument; got a good half hour, and his take.

'If offence isn't meant by those singing the word Yid, and if none is taken by those towards whom it is sung, then how can racial hatred be involved? You are importing a third party into the situation which isn't necessarily there.'

According to this view, certainly those singing Yid Army in support of Spurs are not motivated by racial hatred. Stephen

Pollard is generous enough to allow that it is also possible for many of the opposing fans using the term not to be motivated by racial hatred. In this I think he's right; not everyone is politically involved in the meaning of language. He does accept that use of the words by Tottenham fans 'gives others an argument that it's OK in general use. It's not an argument I agree with, but it is made'.

Somewhere within this debate are the Tottenham chants from the 1990s about Jurgen Klinsmann and Nayim, as in 'Chim Chimeree, Chim Chimeree, Chim Chim Cheroo – Jurgen was a German but now he's a Jew' and its counterpart 'Nayim was an Arab but now he's a Jew'. These songs were meant to welcome the foreign players into the family of Tottenham. It may seem odd to outsiders, and you can still argue that it's harmful, but that doesn't change the intent.

The Auschwitz song, however, can be only on one side, and only defended by those who think the Holocaust is funny. On balance, I think the use of the word by Spurs fans emboldens their rivals to perpetuate it. It would be better to drop it and clarify that its misuse is up there with the N word. Some Spurs fans will howl with anger, but, for me, from now on, it's the Y word and the 'Y*d Army.'

We've come a long way since 1974, a year in which the Burnley chairman Bob Lord banned television cameras, on the grounds that he would 'stand up against a move to get soccer on the cheap by the Jews', but we've still got some way to go.

* * *

Our attitudes to homosexuality have also changed, although again there is some way still to go before homophobic bullying and other forms of abuse are eradicated. However, as with anti-Semitism, homophobia can still be found in the stadiums, albeit rarely. And, as with anti-Semitism, even people who are homophobic know that, in most areas of public discourse, even casual homophobic remarks are no more acceptable to increasing numbers of people than are the anti-Semitic ones.

The one place where homophobia is seen on a regular basis is at Brighton FC. This is because of Brighton's reputation as the 'gay capital' of the UK. Hence the homophobic chant by away fans at the Amex Stadium on Village Way – 'We can see you holding hands', 'Does your boyfriend know you're here?' and, if Brighton is facing relegation (a frequent occurrence) – 'Down with your boyfriend, you're going down with your boyfriend'. One of the words in this chant is sometimes changed. However much these songs have a basis in homophobia, they lack the sheer cruelty and viciousness of many homophobic chants and, on the whole, are sung without malice. It's also possible that a number of those singing may be gay.

Homophobia is one of the new frontiers in prejudice in football. In twenty years it may be considered in the same light as racism, but that depends on how British society changes. Here's how it has already changed, to an extent, and how attitudes can follow on from law. I took a flight to Majorca recently en route to Magaluf, which, if you like traditional English breakfasts, is a culinary paradise. A group of lads boarded the plane. One of them was gay, not camp, but gay enough to tell. He was also one of the lads. They were bantering away, when one of the gang said to him as a put down, 'Yeah, but you like blokes.' In this one sentence was the sea change in Britain since the 1950s. His friends not only accept him as he is, they can tease him as a friend about it. Why? Because they didn't really care. This doesn't mean the modern UK is a paradise of equality where people can 'come out' without fear of reprisal, but perhaps even twenty years ago the group would not have accepted the man, never mind teased him as a friend. You might argue that his sexuality should not be mentioned and you might even be right, but to me it sounded like progress. This may not be typical, and gay men still face prejudice, but the situation is not as bad as it was just two decades ago.

How far still to go? In football, a very long way. Former Chelsea player Graeme Le Saux knows this and he's not even gay. I've never met Le Saux, but I have an affinity with him based on occasionally reading the *Guardian* as a young man and consequently being called gay. This was in what I call my 'Blue Period' or, less artistically, when I was in the RAF. Had I been an officer it might, just, have been acceptable to read this bastion of liberal prejudice, but I wasn't, therefore, obviously, I was gay.

Le Saux tells it better in his autobiography, *Left Field: A Footballer Apart*:

> The *Guardian* was used as one of the most powerful symbols of how I was supposed to be weirdly different. Pathetic, really. It gave substance to the gossip that I was homosexual: *Guardian* reader equals gay boy. Some people really thought that.

The dressing-room gossip filtered through to the terraces:

> 'Le Saux takes it up the a***,' they yelled, again and again. I stood in shock. 'Oh my God, that's it,' I thought. I knew fans everywhere were going to make my life a misery.
>
> Justin Fashanu had 'come out' a year earlier and even though his career was practically over, he was ridiculed

and scorned for his admission. A few years later, he committed suicide [. . .] I do not think a modern footballer could come out as gay without immediately becoming isolated from his team. The group would be too hostile for him to survive [. . .] Suddenly, all the anger and prejudice hidden away under the surface of everyday life starts spewing out of them. You get a sense of the mentality of the mob. If the game starts badly they will turn their anger and their frustration on you.

Most visiting support at Brighton includes a section who will sing the 'holding hands'-type song, but fewer now would subject a player to the sort of abuse Le Saux suffered.

However, some fans from northern clubs will happily use the cosmopolitan atmosphere of the town to further their prejudices about the effete south. Some may even take the Mahmoud Ahmadinejad approach to homosexuality. The former president said there were no gays in Iran. Some of the less informed folks down in Brighton for the weekend might argue there are no homosexuals north of Shrewsbury FC's former home, Gay Meadow. (Shrewsbury now play at the New Meadow – which is much less gay.)

*   *   *

Almost gone from most stadium chants are those about 'Munich 58', concerning the Munich Air Disaster that killed twenty-three people, including eight players and three staff from the hugely talented Manchester United team of 1958. Also seldom heard sung by large numbers of people are chants about the Hillsborough Disaster of 1989 in which ninety-six Liverpool fans died.

Exceptions to this remain, occasionally in the stadium, and more frequently in the pubs around Old Trafford, some of which on match day resound to 'You used to sing Munich – but not any more. Since ninety-six Scousers lay dead on the floor'. Whoever made this one up, and the guys who came up with the others, probably think they have an affinity with their heroes on the pitch and the club staff. Read on a few pages till you get to the bit illustrating what the players think, then think again. When you insult your opponents with that level of abuse, you are insulting the integrity of your own club.

The hypocrisy of a small number of Man Utd and Liverpool fans towards each other is as infuriating as it is nauseating. In one breath they are full of disgust and self-righteous anger towards the other for their taunting of the dead, in the next they are behaving in the same way. The Munich chants, especially at Leeds United ('Who's that dying on the runway?'), began to fade about ten years ago. You can still hear them, occasionally at a ground, occasionally in a pub, but thankfully, as we grow up, less and less.

Some Leeds supporters display the same hypocrisy as the Man Utd and Liverpool fans. They express disgust, for example, at the references to the murder of Leeds fans Christopher Loftus and Kevin Speight in Istanbul in 2000. A few Millwall fans bring Turkish flags along when they play Leeds and sing 'Always look out for Turks carrying knives' to the 'Always Look On the Bright Side of Life' Monty Python tune. But some of those outraged Leeds fans will go on to sing Munich songs. Logic and kindness are not the most prominent characteristics of these people.

Most football fans have got no time for the really vicious stuff. In 2001, Lee Bowyer, then of Leeds United, was found not guilty at Leeds Crown Court on a charge of beating Rotherham student

Sarfraz Najeib unconscious outside a nightclub. At the next away game in which he played, a small group of Leeds fans – about twelve of them – tried to start a racist chant celebrating the whole sorry affair. The several thousand other Leeds fans didn't join in, and dozens turned round and stared at the twelve in disgust. I'm guessing that now, if a similar incident went to court, fans wouldn't even try to start the chant. I may be wrong. I hope not.

I've heard it argued that the gentrification of the game is part of the explanation for the relative reduction in racist and other abusive chants. This is not the case. Industrial-strength language remains commonplace. Thousands of Leeds fans cheerfully joined in a song for Kasper Schmeichel based on the fact that he was the Leeds goalkeeper but his father, Peter, had kept goal for Manchester United: 'Your Dad's a cunt – but you're all right'. Naturally, when he left Leeds, but returned as the Leicester City keeper, the chant changed to 'Your Dad's a cunt – and so are you'. This particular stanza is also aimed at the manager Darren Ferguson, whose dad is Sir Alex Ferguson. Falkirk came up with a good-natured chant for Schmeichel junior – 'I bet your Dad looks good on the dance floor'. This is in the fine tradition of simply having a communal laugh. I'm betting even Kasper smiled, and the players enjoy this aspect of the game, not as much as the fans, but they enjoy it.

British players mostly come from the same backgrounds as the fans. In the dressing rooms the north/south, English/Scottish, Geordie/Mackem divisions and others are all played out, and just as most of the fans know the limits, so do the players, probably more so.

Nigel Spackman had many years at the top of the game playing for Chelsea, Liverpool and other clubs before a spell in management. He's now one of the new generation of astute, intelligent media football analysts who look at the game as a whole, not just at what happens on the pitch. He's got no time for the racist or otherwise fully offensive songs, but agrees: the players are aware of them and of the funny ones.

> Some of the songs you do hear. You'd be warming up, or there might be stop in play and you hear them more clearly, and you think 'That's very clever'. We don't really talk about them too much as a team, but among your own social group, within or outside the team, you might, especially the funny ones.
>
> However, when it comes to racism I have to say that the vast majority of footballers don't relate to those songs whatsoever. If your own supporters are singing racist stuff, or about a tragedy and you know what they're on about, then everyone agrees it's not right, it's disrespectful, distasteful, to yourself and your club. We know that in our world, our lives, these were terrible moments and the fans need to show respect.
>
> We're now in a world where you have to look at racism, at sexual orientation, and yes you've got to understand football humour, but you've got to understand there are limits, you've got to understand wider society.

He told me a sad, funny story of humour and racism which is a brilliant example of the unseen lines being approached, crossed, bent and subverted.

> When I was with Chelsea, we were at Rangers, at Ibrox, for a charity match to raise money after the Bradford fire

disaster. I didn't know the whole Protestant/Catholic thing up there at the time, but we had a couple of black players, and one of them was subbed. A few Rangers fans booed him and we think it was because he was black, but then Phillip Priest came on to replace him and the whole ground broke out booing because of his name and calling for the first guy to be brought back on.

Nigel was quick to recognise that the first round of booing was by a minority and not funny, the second was widespread and a joke. The foundation of that joke is indeed sectarian, but it is not necessarily born of malevolence. He agreed that British society has changed. We are not as racist nor as unthinking about humanity as we were, and those of us who are, know to keep it to themselves most of the time, except when they gather enough numbers to feel they can get away with it.

To people with emotional intelligence, and a heart, Munich, Ibrox, Hillsborough, Bradford, Heysel and the other tragedies all involved real people, with real lives and real families. And to those who don't possess such faculties? To those few in The Kop chanting 'Munich 58', to those at the Stretford End chanting about Hillsborough, and those at Millwall waving Turkish flags at Leeds supporters because two fans were murdered by thugs from Galatasaray in Istanbul? They should bear in mind that if 100 of them are singing something pathetic, most of the other 40,000, 30,000, or even 10,000 of us think they are yesterday's losers and not proper fans.

Here's an example of why: Everton fans venturing into Yorkshire have been known to chant 'Yorkshire police – murderers' at the thin blue line before them. This is a direct reference to the Hillsborough disaster and in solidarity with their usually loathed red cousins across Stanley Park. Leave to one side the veracity of the chant, the point is that, for the sake of Merseyside, they can put aside their differences. On all the other examples I cite – Heysel, Galatasaray, etc. – most of us are decent enough to put aside our differences for the sake of humanity. It's really not very hard.

And what of Bobby von Dazzler and Ernst Strongman in our apocryphal north/south grudge match?

Bobby had told the ref that his leg was broken in two places and his metatarsal had fractured, but the doctor sprayed his shin with a magic solution, and lo! he leaped to his feet and scored from the free kick. Ten minutes later, Ernst received a straight red card for elbowing Bobby in the head, which according to the Newcastle fans was unfair given that it was accidental, and anyway was the correct thing to do, given that the cheating soft southern bastard had gone down too easily in the first place.

Second Half

If You Know
Your History

Captain John Currie Lauder of the 1st/8th Battalion, Argyll and Sutherland Highlanders, was killed in action on 28 December 1916 on the Somme. Army records state that he was killed by a sniper's bullet. It is said his dying words to his troops were 'Carry on'. A century later, a song written in his memory is sung by thousands of Birmingham City fans. 'Keep Right On to the End of the Road' is the club's signature tune, a genuine anthem, and it's theirs and theirs alone. No other fans sing it. It is as much a part of Birmingham City Football Club as 'On the Ball, City!' is part of Norwich City. The song is Scottish in its roots, and although its Scottish connection to Birmingham is not direct, it is fitting that the club plays at St Andrews.

Captain Lauder's father was Sir Harry Lauder from Edinburgh. In 1917, the grieving father, a former miner who had become a massively popular music-hall star, wrote the song in tribute to his son. It was one of the best-known songs of its time, and Lauder senior closed most of his shows with it until his death in 1950. It is a paean to John, to the hope of being reunited with him in heaven, and to keeping faith in God no matter what blows life hits you with. In this respect at least, it is fitting that Birmingham City fans adopted it, as supporting the Blues has been a long sorry tale of the club from England's second city, doomed, seemingly for ever, to be mostly in the country's second division.

Of course this pain pales alongside that of a father losing his son, but there is something behind the passion of the fans which echoes the passion of Harry Lauder, and it is a unique tribute to a soldier of the First World War. For that alone, Lauder's song is worth repeating in full as we approach the centenary of Captain John Currie Lauder's death, at the age of 25.

Ev'ry road thro' life is a long, long road,
Fill'd with joys and sorrows too,
As you journey on how your heart will yearn
For the things most dear to you.
With wealth and love 'tis so,
But onward we must go.

Keep right on to the end of the road,
Keep right on to the end,
Tho' the way be long, let your heart be strong,
Keep right on round the bend.
Tho' you're tired and weary still journey on,
Till you come to your happy abode,
Where all the love you've been dreaming of
Will be there at the end of the road.

With a big stout heart to a long steep hill,
We may get there with a smile,
With a good kind thought and an end in view,
We may cut short many a mile.
So let courage ev'ry day
Be your guiding star always.

Birmingham City fans have changed some of the words, but in essence it is Lauder's song they sing. The story of how it ended up on the terraces is part of Blues fans' folklore.

In January 1956, the Birmingham City coach was en route to Leyton Orient for an FA Cup fourth round tie. It was not unusual in those days for the players to have a singsong on the coach, and when manager Arthur Turner asked City's Scottish winger Alex Govan to give them a tune, he came up with a rendition of Lauder's classic. The team won four–nil, the singsong became obligatory, and Govan's choice became the team's favourite.

A few weeks later they were at Arsenal for the quarter final. An article on the Birmingham City FC website quotes Govan's memories of the day:

Arthur Turner shouted 'Let's have one from Scotland, Alex'. I duly obliged with 'Keep Right On to the End of the Road' once again. This time some of the other lads joined in the chorus and one by one they quickly caught on to the words. We sang it again and again until the entire coach was rocking as we pulled up outside Highbury!

I remember the coach was one of the older types which had wind down windows alongside the seats. It was a warm day so all the lads had their windows down and with the strains of 'Keep Right On . . .' going at full belt, the Blues fans who always congregated outside the ground to welcome us to away games could hear us coming several streets away!

They picked up on the words too and were all singing it as we filed off the coach. The rest, as they say, is history!

Captain John Currie Lauder is buried at the Ovilliers Military Cemetery on the Somme. You can find his grave in Plot I, Row A, Grave 6.

* * *

Not every Birmingham City fan will know the background to their signature song, nor will many fans of other clubs know theirs. That level of detail is not the central thing here, although a solid grasp of it does add even more to what fans do think is important, and that is the sense of ownership of the song, and therefore of belonging.

All football fans are magpies. They will take songs from anywhere. Nursery rhymes, advertising jingles, TV theme tunes, hymns, folksongs, opera, music-hall, pop songs, national anthems and films have all been used, for better or worse. When a particular song becomes identified with a particular club, it is rare for other supporters to try to adopt it. However, if it's a free for all, then songs are a bit like fashion in the way that they spread.

I think the central argument in the film *The Devil Wears Prada* is flawed. The character played by Meryl Streep waxes lyrical about how the poor benighted masses think they are making choices about what to wear, but in fact are reacting to what the elite choose to push upon them. This is not the case. A lot of fashion comes from the street, is adopted by the designers, and is then returned in a more widespread manner. Most football songs make a similar journey, but remove the middle man. A song is heard one week, copied the next, and within a few weeks has spread throughout the land.

Some have a shelf life of only a few seasons, others go on for decades. 'You're gonna get your fucking heads kicked in' lasted about ten years and then, along with 'You're going home in a fucking ambulance', just faded away. How endearing and quaint they seem now. Then there are songs that are both perennial and ubiquitous: 'We're gonna win the League/Cup/Inter Toto Shield' (delete as applicable) get run out each spring from whichever club still harbours hope of success that season. But the signature song is usually unique.

Almost every club has a signature song of sorts. Some are reluctantly shared, for example Nottingham Forest fans are one of several to borrow one of Paul McCartney's most famous tunes. They replace 'Mull of Kintyre' with 'City Ground', and the song becomes:

Oh City Ground;
Far have I travelled and much have I seen
Goodison and Anfield are the places I've been.
Maine Road and Old Trafford still echo the sound
Of the boys in the red from the City Ground.
City Ground, Oh mist rolling in from the Trent,
My desire is always to be here.
Oh City Ground.

'You'll Never Walk Alone' is (famously) the signature tune for Liverpool FC, though in recent years this has been challenged by

'Fields of Anfield Road' and 'Poor Tommy Scouser'. The former is sung to the tune of 'Fields of Athenry', an Irish folksong from the 1970s about the Great Famine in Ireland in the 1840s, also known as the Irish potato famine. In the original, by Pete St John, the words to the chorus are 'Low lie the Fields of Athenry':

Where once we watched the small free birds fly.
Our love was on the wing we had dreams and songs
to sing
It's so lonely 'round the Fields of Athenry.

The Liverpool version takes the tune, the basics of the original, and comes up with something which, at full volume on a feverish European night at Anfield, with the flags flying and scarves aloft, is a sight to behold and a sound that explains why God put hairs on the back of your neck:

Outside the Shankly Gates
I heard a Kopite calling:
Shankly! they have taken you away . . .
But you left a great eleven
Before you went to heaven
Now it's glory round the Fields of Anfield Road.

All round the Fields of Anfield Road
Where once we watched the King Kenny play (and he
could play)
We had Heighway on the wing
We had dreams and songs to sing
Of the glory round the Fields of Anfield Road

Outside the Paisley Gates
I heard a Kopite calling
Paisley! they have taken you away . . .
You led the great eleven
Back in Rome in '77
And the Redmen they are still playing the same way

All round the Fields of Anfield Road
Where once we watched the King Kenny play (and he
  could play)
We had Heighway on the wing
We had dreams and songs to sing
Of the glory round the Fields of Anfield Road.

Celtic fans sing the original, as do fans of the Irish national side, which has contributed to the confusion over whether Liverpool and Everton were originally Protestant or Catholic clubs. In fact, they both grew out of shared Methodist beginnings and there was nothing sectarian about the split in the 1890s. The St Domingo Methodist church in the Everton district had a cricket team, which became a football team, which grew into Everton FC. The players and officials used to meet at a local hotel next to 'Ye Anciente Everton Toffee House', and this led to the club's nickname of 'The Toffees'. (Lucky the hotel wasn't located next to Aunt Annie's Whore House.)

Anyway, a bitter row within the club involving money, beer, land and ego resulted in the historic split of 1892. Former club president and mayor of the city, John Houlding, formed Liverpool FC, and each club set up shop on different sides of Stanley Park. The rivalry was instant (which was helpful, as it did away with any need for a series of events over decades to develop a lasting enmity). Everton win the 'Who is oldest' competition, but Liverpool fans benefit from not having to explain to people where they are from.

Social historian David Kennedy, in his work *Red and Blue and Orange and Green?*, has shown how the political affiliations of some of the directors of the clubs in the subsequent years contributed to the idea that one was Catholic and the other Protestant, but I've yet to see solid evidence that, on a religious level, one leant one way or the other. Their scouting networks were different, and Everton recruited more players from Ireland in the first half of the twentieth century, but at a fan level, in what is a very mixed city, with a large number of people descended from Irish and Northern Irish heritage, there appears to be no difference.

This is certainly true in our age. The 'Fields of Anfield Road' has a solid Irish Catholic connection, while the second half of 'Poor Tommy Scouser' is sung to a tune straight out of the Protestant side of Belfast – 'The Sash My Father Wore' – commemorating the victory of William of Orange in 1690–91. The first half is sung to 'Red River Valley', an American folksong from the 1880s, first recorded in the 1920s by the cowboy singer Carl T. Sprague. How it made its way over here and onto the terraces is unclear. It has featured in several films between the 1930s and 1960s, some of which were shown in the UK, and it was used as a marching song by British paratroopers in the Second World War. Somehow, somewhere, someone sat down in the 1960s, changed the lyrics completely, took them to The Kop and began a tradition which is pure Liverpool:

Can I tell you the story of a poor boy
Who was sent far away from his home

To fight for his king and his country
And also the old folks back home.

Now they put him in a Highland division
Sent him off to a far foreign land
Where the flies flew around in their thousands
And there's nothing to see but the sand

Well the battle started next morning
Under the Libyan sun
I remember that poor Scouser Tommy
Who was shot by an old Nazi gun

As he lay on the battle field dying (dying dying)
With blood gushing out of his head
As he lay on the battle field dying (dying dying)
These were the last words he said . . .

Ohhhhhh . . . I am a Liverpudlian
I come from the Spion Kop
I love to sing, I love to shout
I go there quite a lot
We support the team that's dressed in Red
It's the team that you all know
It's the team that we call Liverpool
And to glory we will go.

Since 1982 an extra verse has been added to revel in the five–nil thrashing of Everton, which included four goals by Ian Rush. The first lines are sung to 'Puff the Magic Dragon' and the last lines are sung to the tune of 'All You Need Is Love':

> *We've won the League, we've won the Cup*
> *And we've been to Europe too*
> *We played the toffees for a laugh*
> *And we left them feeling blue – Five–Nil!*

> *One two, One two three*
> *One two three four, Five–Nil!*

> *Rush scored one, Rush scored two, Rush scored three,*
> *   And Rush scored four*
> *All you need is Rush, da da dah da dah,*
> *All you need is Rush, da da dah da dah,*
> *All you need is Rush, Rush. Rush is all you need.*

The cathedral for these songs is Anfield, and the choir is in the Spion Kop. Many of us call the stand behind the home end in our stadiums the Kop, but only Liverpool's is 'The Kop'. If you doubt this, think of any conversation between football fans of several different clubs – if someone mentions The Kop, we all know which one they are talking about.

The word kop comes from the Boer War and the Boer word for hill. In 1900, on Tuesday, 23 January, soldiers from the First Battalion of the South Lancashire Regiment, the Second Battalion Lancashire Fusiliers and the Second Battalion of the Royal Lancaster Regiment assembled at the bottom of a hill that the Boers called Spion Kop, or Spy Hill, near the town of Ladysmith. The British took the hill in thick fog almost unopposed. When the fog lifted, they realised why. Above them was another kop, and on this were the Boer forces. They had a clear line of fire down on to the British, who couldn't even dig proper trenches in the rocky terrain. Over two days the Boers picked off the British forces one by one in an area only slightly bigger than a football pitch. The official records differ, but it is thought at least 332 men were killed and 563 wounded.

The Battle of Spion Kop was a disaster for the British Army and was front-page news back home, the name etched in the public consciousness, at least until 1914. Veterans of the campaign who returned home and saw the steep banking of the cheapest standing areas in stadiums were reminded of the South African hills and began to call them the Kop, and sometimes the Spion Kop.

It's thought the first to be so named was at Woolwich Arsenal in 1904, but when the club moved north of the River Thames to Highbury, the name did not travel with it. Two years later, in the late spring of 1906, Liverpool FC had just won the league and, to build for the future, decided a new standing area was needed at the Walton Breck Road end. At the same time, the council was building a new tram line along the road. The council needed to get rid of the rubble from the construction, the club needed rubble to construct. Like many a game at Anfield, it was a good match.

It is said that local men, veterans of the South Lancashire Regiment, dubbed it the Spion Kop, but the first record of the name is from the then *Liverpool Echo* sports editor, Ernest Edwards (and not Ernest Jones, as is often written). Edwards, despite being a Brummie, grew to love the city of Liverpool. He was concerned about safety at local grounds and felt The Kop had improved matters. His great grandson, Mike Brown, has found an article from 28 September 1906, in which his ancestor writes:

> Thanks to the broad, forceful policy adopted by the go-ahead directors of Liverpool FC, the danger is past, visitors to Anfield, whether on the giddy heights of the Spioenkop or the lowland terraces, can be sure that they are safe.

It is seems doubtful he just came up with the term by himself, and Mr Brown does not claim so. It is more likely Edwards knew of the nickname from covering games at the stadium.

As for the Spion Kop's best-known song? Many people think of 'You'll Never Walk Alone' as 'the old Gerry and the Pacemakers song'. It is, but Gerry Marsden's 1963 popular beat combo version was but the latest in a long line of covers since the 1945 original from the Rogers and Hammerstein musical *Carousel*. (Perhaps this is not quite to the point, but it is worth asking why Gerry gave his group the moniker 'The Pacemakers'. Research suggests Mr Marsden was inspired after watching an athletics meeting and not a heart bypass operation.)

The first recording I've found of 'You'll Never Walk Alone' by Liverpool fans is from a 1964 game. By the 1965 League Cup Final between Liverpool and Leeds, the great commentator Kenneth Wolstenholme is confident enough to name-check it as 'the Liverpool signature tune', and the even greater Liverpool manager Bill Shankly had chosen it as one of his songs on Radio 4's *Desert Island Discs* the month before the final. Wolstenholme was that rarity in football commentating – he knew that just because there was a microphone in front of him, he didn't have to talk into it all the time. During the match he just stopped talking and let the song create the atmosphere, occasionally saying the name of the player on the ball.

The original is an awful saccharine shriek fest, but Frank Sinatra, Judy Garland, the Three Tenors and Elvis Presley are among the many who have tried to do justice to the anthem. However, I don't think anyone has ever captured the spirit of the song like The Kop, especially in the dark days after Hillsborough, in memory of the ninety-six.

*   *   *

To be human is to sing. We've always done it. All recorded history shows evidence that we have been musical since we have been human, and I'll wager we were singing in prehistory, and not just when we were winning. It has been used to bond groups, whether round the camp-fire in the village, or the camp-fire above the battleground for the next day's fight.

All cultures sing and we all sing in different ways at different times: at funerals, at weddings, in the pub, round the fire, in church, mosque, temple and on the terraces. The Maoris sing, the Welsh sing, the Massed Choir of the Democratic People's Republic of Korea sings, even Fulham fans sing. Occasionally. Born-again Christians sing loudly, the Catholics sing movingly, the Methodists sing soberly, and the Church of England mumbles to itself quietly in a very friendly, non-threatening way, in case anyone thinks all of its senior clergy might actually believe in the Virgin Birth and the divinity of Jesus.

And we sing on the terraces. Once upon a time we only sang on Saturday afternoons. Now it might be at Saturday lunchtime, to limit the alcohol intake before a local derby match, or on Sunday afternoon, to give us time to warm up our tonsils in church, or not. It might be Monday or Wednesday evening, or even, if we are really unfortunate, Thursday evening, but sing we do, and we love it. The signature song of a club brings with it a wealth of emotions. 'Blue Moon', 'Bubbles', even that mournful super-slow 'When the Spurs Go Marching In' at White Hart Lane, bring that sense of identity.

If that identity causes you to kick someone in the head, then you're a lettuce-leaf short of a salad. For the rest of us who also live in an increasingly atomised society, the identification is positive. Monty Python took on the group-think of 'Yes, we're all individuals' in the film *Life of Brian*. It satirised the unthinking conformity of allowing religion to tell you how to live your life without questioning it. Football has indeed been called a religion, and the snobs look down on fans as being as sheep-like as some of the religious. The snobs don't know us. The snobs take it too seriously, but then again, so do those who aren't the full salad.

Yes, it's passion, albeit not of the magnitude of Easter; yes, it's conformity, but communal singing, especially of the signature songs, goes deep into what connects us as well as what divides us. Don't get me wrong. When singing 'You'll Never Walk Alone', the Koppites are not simultaneously thinking 'Ah yes, this is me fulfilling my primal need to come together with my tribe and demonstrate that I'll be there for them, and I know they are there for me'. However, there is something of that going on, and the idea attributed to Mrs Thatcher that there is no such thing as society is so wrong.

We are now more apart than ever before from our extended families, despite there being an expensive transport system to help us connect with each other. We don't go to church any more; the local shops have often closed, so off we go to the MetroCentre, Bluewater or the Bullring. We often live and work in different places, and hey, it's not that bad. But – we are social animals (some are just animals), and we choose to socialise in a football stadium.

These are the places we may have been going to for decades, or just a few years. The ground may have changed. Where you used to stand as a kid is now seated, the old scratching shed may now be a modern stand with a Sainsbury's built on to the back, but it's still a shared home. You know you belong, and apart from bellowing racist abuse or contorting your face like a monkey and throwing coins at Wayne Rooney, you are welcome.

Unless you're with a group of fellow season ticket holders, the person to one side of you may be a complete stranger, but turning to them and engaging in conversation is not considered strange. Well, as long as it's football related. You don't want to start asking if they saw *The Andrew Marr Show* last week, or if they think the UK has a chance in this year's Eurovision Song Contest. However, suggesting that manager Joseph Morewhineo has dropped Bobby von Dazzler because the newspaper reports that he was out on the town with two women and ten drinks are correct, is quite acceptable.

Being Billy No Mates at a game can be difficult. As I don't live in the city of my upbringing, I'm sometimes at home and away games on my own, not having been able to get tickets with the guys I've been with in the pub beforehand. Now, if you went to the cinema or a restaurant on your own and engaged in a conversation with a neighbour, you'd probably get short shrift. In the ground, most people will have a chat, but a few clearly wonder why you're on your own.

I remember an excruciatingly embarrassing day in 2010 when I had two tickets to a home game, but my friend Ben England couldn't make it. I sold the spare, at less than face value, to a seemingly desperate guy outside the stadium who said he only had a tenner on him but he just had to get in. Thirty minutes later he showed up next to me stinking of ale, and carrying a large meat pie, a bar of Cadbury's and a coffee, none of which he offered me. Happily there was room elsewhere and I moved. Anyway, apart from him, even if you've only exchanged grunts of 'Al reet?', 'Awright?' or 'Eh up' when the signature song begins, any differences are forgotten (except for mean pie man – I make an exception for him), and the congregation rises.

There's something deeply satisfying about communal singing. Just ask any passing Welsh person at an Eisteddfod. You add your one voice to the many, and each voice is as important as the other. You create something you can hear, not see, but you can feel it.

* * *

But not all songs are full of 'long steep hills' and 'guiding stars'. It is perfectly possible to have a song of pride in local identity which is simultaneously heartfelt and tongue in cheek. Sheffield United fans provide a good example with their take on John Denver's 'Annie's Song', or 'You Fill Up My Senses', as most of us know it. It is a tribute to the good things in life: tobacco, beer, chip butties and your local team. Before you learn the words and join the Blades fans behind the goal on the Shoreham – a few translations. Woodbines are the unfiltered industrial-strength cigarettes known locally as 'gaspers'. They are still to be found in a corner shop near you at a price you think you can afford if you're a smoker and can't afford Marlboro, even though there is actually little difference. There was a time when you could buy a packet of five Woodbines, but if you were really on your uppers, you could always find a newsagent who sold Park Drive in singles. Well, I could anyway.

Magnet is a John Smith's bitter (4 per cent ABV), much beloved of many a citizen of Sheffield. It had been brewed in

Tadcaster, North Yorkshire, since the late nineteenth century, where the hard water contributed, it is said, to its 'subtle balance of bitter-sweet flavours; caramel and a hint of liquorice . . . ' However, Heineken, hitherto unknown for its expertise in making northern English bitter, bought the brand and moved the brewery sixty-five miles north to Hartlepool, whereupon some drinkers declared it not to be the same pint and gave it up. Not, however, many folk in Sheffield, who, to this day, will travel several miles to find a pub still selling it. Given that I am still in mourning for the withdrawal from the UK of an ultra fizzy American lager known as Rolling Rock, best drunk ice cold so you can't taste it, I am in no position to judge the attractions of Magnet, but the song's a good 'un:

You fill up my senses,
Like a gallon of Magnet,
Like a packet of Woodbines,
Like a good pinch of snuff,
Like a night out in Sheffield,
Like a greasy chip butty,
Like Sheffield United,
Come fill me again.

Michael Palin, of Monty Python and travelling-around-the-world fame, may well have sung this, as he is a Sheffield United fan. He may also have sung the other Sheffield club's 'Honolulu Wednesday' (see over), as he professes allegiance to Wednesday as well. This is bizarre behaviour, which he puts down to an affinity with the city. I put it down to him being a Python, so that logical absurdities don't mean to him what they mean to you and me. Because of this, perhaps we can forgive him for the heresy of supporting two rival clubs, but I doubt fans of United and Wednesday do.

Boston United fans have their own version of 'You Fill Up My Senses', which refers to the local family-owned brewery Batemans, Lincolnshire crisp-company Pipers, and that fine accompaniment to both, the pickled egg:

You fill up my senses,
Like a gallon of Batemans,
Like a packet of Seasalt,
Like a good pickled egg,
Like a night out in Boston,
Like a greasy chip butty,
Like Boston United,
Come fill me again.

All of the above songs indicate, in their different ways, why a major British bank showed it simply didn't understand football fans when, in 2004, it launched a competition to find England's Chant Laureate. This idea can only have come from a marketing department staffed by people who had never gone through a turnstile.

The Poet Laureate title goes back to at least King James I who, in 1617, thought Ben Jonson could pen an ode or two. Some scholars believe it goes further back, to Chaucer and the 1300s. Either way, it is a fine, indeed noble, idea, and some of the country's greatest lines have been knocked out by many a Poet Laureate, including Wordsworth and Tennyson. If you put your mind to it, and the muse took you, you could probably rework 'I wandered lonely as a cloud' into a chant, but the Poet Laureate is the Poet Laureate and we simply don't need a Chant Laureate – we already have hundreds of them happily scribbling away in pubs the length and breadth of the country.

Anyway, the prize was won by 37-year-old Birmingham City fan Jonny Hurst with a song hymning praise to an Aston Villa player. Now, I've nothing against Mr Hurst, he may well be a talented writer, and congratulations for winning, but a Chant Laureate? Aston Villa? Who writes a song praising their closest rivals? Mr Hurst received the £10,000 winner's prize and got to tour Premier League stadiums, where he was greeted politely by club officials and considered an irrelevance by club fans.

One of the judges who voted for Mr Hurst was the Poet Laureate Andrew Motion, who said, 'What we felt we were tapping into was a huge reservoir of folk poetry'. Yes, indeed. And since when did folk poetry come from corporate bankers? As far as is known, the sea shanties of this island, the ancient nursery rhymes remembering the Black Death, the regimental songs of the military and the old songs from the countryside were not brought to you by Lloyds of London, Barclays, NatWest or any other financial institution. Happily, the bankers in question swallowed their prawn sandwiches, did not continue with their folly, and have actually now tuned in to where we come from in order to better sell their wares. Chant Laureate? Give over! Next, Man Utd will come up with the idea of a 'singing section' for the stadium . . . No, wait.

*   *   *

Jonny Hurst had a difficult gig. If Elgar couldn't get a song going, what hope did Jonny have? Yes, that Elgar. Sir Edward Elgar – turns out he was a bit of an enigma. His claim to fame is partially down to writing the tune to 'Land of Hope and Glory'; less well known are his efforts in 1898, at Wolverhampton Wanderers' ground,

Molineux, to get the crowd to sing one of his compositions. You can imagine the scene. High up behind the goal Sir Edward is hoisted onto a crash barrier, arms spread wide, chest puffed out, as he bellows at the away fans 'You're going home in a horse-drawn ambulance'.

I am indebted to Wolves fan Henry Palfrey for that chant, and his follow up, 'Come on a penny farthing, you must have come on a penny farthing'. To this, I can only add that upon sight of the away fans, he may have led a spirited chant of 'Who art thou?' The route to Elgar's song 'He Banged the Leather for Goal' is more prosaic, but does involve a bicycle.

Elgar was a late convert to the beautiful game, attending his first match in 1898, at the age of forty, when he went to see Wolves v. Stoke City. He'd become fascinated with football through his friendship with a woman named Dora Penny, who lived close to Molineux. In her book, *Edward Elgar: Memories of a Variation*, she writes: 'I quickly found out that music was the last thing he wanted to talk about [. . .] he wanted to know if I ever saw Wolverhampton Wanderers play and when he heard that our house was a stone's throw from their ground he was quite excited.'

Elgar used to cycle from Malvern to Wolverhampton, which is quite a feat in itself, and then accompany Ms Penny to Molineux. She remembers: 'The dense crowd flowing down the road like a river, the roar of welcome as the rival teams came on to the ground [. . .] and the deafening roar that greeted a goal [. . .] it all delighted him.'

After his first game, Elgar asked Ms Penny to send him a cutting of the match report. A striker named Billy Malpas had scored, and in the write-up, the journalist described how Malpas had 'banged the leather for goal'. 'I'll have that,' said Elgar, or words to that effect, and penned three bars of music to go with his lyrics – 'We'll bang the leather for goal – we'll bang the leather for goal'. Alas, for the man who came up with the *Enigma Variations*, the song failed to catch on and has not been passed down the generations. However, perhaps Mr Elgar would smile if he knew that to this day, every Saturday, to the tune of his 'Land of Hope and Glory', thousands of people sing 'We hate Nottingham Forest, we hate Liverpool too. And Leicester!' No one's quite sure why 'And Leicester!' was added to this song in the late 1960s because, unless we are from Derby, Nottingham, or possibly Coventry, we don't. Well, not especially.

In 1898, *The Times* was quite sniffy about Elgar's attempt at becoming a terrace legend, doubting it would catch on and believing that 'the melody may be complex for the Grandstand'. Bloody cheek! We've managed to get our vocal cords around Giuseppe Verdi's 'La donna è mobile' from *Rigoletto*, for example, with 'Your ground's too big for you'. I'm sure the Wolves fans could have handled three bars of Elgar.

After it was played for the first time in public (2010), Christopher Morley of the *Birmingham Post* described the three bars as having 'a dramatic phrase involving a descending minor ninth over excitable tremolandi in the accompaniment, with a crashing downward flourish'. A bit like 'Your ground's too big for you', then. Tom Kelly of the Elgar Society tells me he tried his hand at it, 'but it's not easy to sing as a solo or as a terrace ensemble', so it's just as well Sir Elgar didn't give up the day job. Dora Penny comes out of the tale quite well. By way of thanks for introducing him to the delights of Wolverhampton Wanderers FC, Elgar wrote 'Dorabella' as part of his famous *Enigma Variations* in 1899. Which was nice.

'He Banged the Leather for Goal' has the same feel about it as a song written more or less at the same time, but in Norwich, and adopted by Norwich City fans in 1902. 'On the Ball, City!' may be pure Victorian 'Play up and play the game', but it has survived to this day and shows no signs of fading. It also retains, from football's lexicon, the word scrimmage. You won't find many football conversations which include the words 'that was a good scrimmage', but Norfolk's finest have kept the word alive.

In the days to call, which we have left behind,
Our boyhood's glorious game,
And our youthful vigour has declined
With its mirth and its lonesome end;
You will think of the time, the happy time,
Its memories fond recall
When in the bloom of your youthful prime
We've kept upon the ball.

Kick off, throw in, have a little scrimmage,
Keep it low, a splendid rush, bravo, win or die;
On the ball, City, never mind the danger,
Steady on, now's your chance,
Hurrah! We've scored a goal.

Let all tonight then drink with me
To the football game we love,
And wish it may successful be
And in one grand united toast
Join player, game and song

And fondly pledge your pride and toast
Success to the City club.

Kick off, throw in, have a little scrimmage,
Keep it low, a splendid rush, bravo, win or die;
On the ball, City, never mind the danger,
Steady on, now's your chance,
Hurrah! We've scored a goal.

You've got to love this song. 'Hurrah! We've scored a goal.' It is hopelessly dated, quaint, and sounds as if it was written by the Hugh Laurie character, Lieutenant The Hon. George Colthurst St Barleigh, in *Blackadder Goes Forth*. Nowadays, Norwich City fans only sing the chorus, but with such gusto they honour their team and the composer Albert T. Smith who, in 1905, was made a director of the club. It's a local song for a community club, and entirely the better for it. Well done, chaps, carry on.

Norwich claim 'On the Ball, City!' as the oldest football song in Britain. They may be right, but have to argue their case against some Newcastle United supporters who point out that 'Blaydon Races' was written a good thirty years before the Norwich anthem. The riposte to that is simple: 'Blaydon Races' is a song about going to see a horse race, not a football match. Even so, it's a cracking tale, written in 1862 by George Ridley, a former boy miner who went on to become a popular entertainer. And it's a good terrace song, taken up by supporters from several clubs – although they have to change the lyrics. Ridley recounts the adventures en route to the races when the wheels come off, but he does bang on a bit; which explains why Newcastle fans, like others, tend mostly to sing only the chorus.

"Dirty Northern Bastards!"

I went to Blaydon Races
'Twas on the ninth of June
Eighteen Hundred and Sixty Two
On a Summer's Afternoon
We took the bus from Balmbras
And she was heavy laden
Away we went along Collingwood Street
That's on the Road to Blaydon

Chorus:
Oh me lads, you should've seen us gannin'
Passing the folks along the road
Just as they were stannin'
Aal the lads and lasses there
Aal wi' smilin' faces
Gannin along the Scotswood Road
To see the Blaydon Races

We flew past Armstrong's factory
And up by the Robin Adair
But gannin ower the Railway Bridge
The bus wheel flew off there
The lasses lost their crinolenes
And the veils that hide their faces
I got two black eyes and a broken nose
Ingannin t' Blaydon Races

Chorus:
Oh me lads ...

Now when we got the wheel back on
Away we went again
But them that had their noses broke
They went back ower hyem
Some went to the dispensary
And some to Doctor Gibbses
And some to the infirmary
To mend their broken ribses

Chorus:
Oh me lads . . .

Now when we got to Paradise
There were bonny games begun
There were four and twenty on the bus
And how we danced and sung
They called on me to sing a song
So I sung 'em 'Paddy Fagan'
I danced a jig and I swung me twig
The day wi' went to Blaydon

Chorus:
Oh me lads . . .

We flew across the Chain Bridge
And into Blaydon Toon
The bellman he was calling then
They called him Jackie Broon
I saw him talking to some chaps
And them he was persuadin'

To gan and see Geordie Ridley's show
At the Mechanics' Hall in Blaydon

Chorus:
Oh me lads...

The rain it poured down all the day
And made the ground quite muddy
Coffee Johnny had a white hat on
Shouted 'Whi stole the cuddy?'
There were spice stalls and monkey shows
And owld wives selling ciders
And a chap on a ha'penny roundaboot
Saying 'noo me lads for riders?'

Chorus:
Oh me lads...

Like I said, George went on a bit, but this is possibly the best example of what is essentially an English folksong, preserved through football. Terrace culture is one of the last ways the oral tradition of some ancient songs and tunes are now passed down through the generations. Folk music had a brief period of being fashionable in the 1960s; Lindisfarne and, later, even Gazza had hits with 'Fog on the Tyne', and although Simon and Garfunkel managed to resurrect 'Scarborough Fair', overall we don't sing the communal songs we used to and they are not part of popular culture.

I was heartened to hear, at the end of the 2013/14 season, that 'Knees Up Mother Brown' is still known to Londoners. On the last day of their season, Brentford (The Bees) were already promoted from League One, playing at home, and the fans were having a party. Then news came through that Fulham, a mere three miles away, were relegated from the Premier League and would be joining them in the Championship. Within minutes the chant went up 'Bees up – Fulham down, Bees up – Fulham down. Bees up, Bees up, don't let the breeze up, Bees up – Fulham down!'

Imagine: if Newcastle fans and others didn't sing versions of 'Blaydon Races', it's likely the song would be lost. As it is, Mr Ridley made quite a journey. I see Bruce Willis in the lead role, if a Hollywood film is ever made of it, and after the 'two black eyes and broken nose' incident he could say, 'Ha'way. I'm too old for this shite'.

The regional rewrites of 'Blaydon Races', such as 'Going down the Warwick Way to see Matt Busby's Aces', are beginning to fade, but the original remains a Geordie classic. It can also be a blessed relief to hear it, as it sometimes break up the tedium of having to listen to ten minutes of uninterrupted 'Toon Army!'

I'm sure the Newcastle fans keep this chant up for what seems like days on end in order to irritate opposition supporters. It works.

* * *

Not all songs have such illustrious histories as 'Blaydon Races'; the story of how Chelsea fans began to sing 'Ten Men Went to Mow' is cutting-edge modern, very silly, and very football.

Opinions are mixed about the man responsible. Mickey Greenaway was a true Blue who for decades led the singing in the Shed End at Stamford Bridge. There was no questioning his passion and commitment, but there are people who say he was also involved in hooliganism. A friend of a friend who used to go to Chelsea games with Greenaway puts him in the 'diamond geezer' category. He says things sometimes 'got a bit naughty' but is adamant that Greenaway was never in the infamous Chelsea 'Headhunters' gang and was a proper fan. Reading his obituaries, one of which calls him a folk hero, it's clear he was not a stalwart member of the Sally Army, but he doesn't sound like one of the psychos.

The friend of a friend says that in the early 1980s, Greenaway was driving to a pre-season game in Sweden with four other fans. Somewhere north of the M25 they realised they hadn't brought any CDs to play. In this version of the tale, a CD of children's songs was found: 'Ten Men Went to Mow' went down very well in the car, so much so that they, along with a few other Chelsea fans, continued singing it in the bars in Sweden. The following week, at another pre-season friendly, but this time at Stamford Bridge, it was being sung in the pubs near the stadium. It was then given a run out during the game, and by the end of the 1981/82 season it had become the most popular song in the Shed End.

Greenaway was a living legend in his Chelsea world, but fell on hard times. He lost his job, was banned from the stadium follow-ing unproven allegations about him in a national newspaper, and died a virtual recluse in a bedsit. In his glory years he also started another Chelsea chant which is now a classic, and one of the bars beneath the stands is named the Zigger Zagger in his memory.

'Ten Men Went to Mow' is a traditional British counting-song for children, teaching them how to count backwards. What's not to like about a song in which you can shout 'Spot!' after the 'and his dog' line and, should the fancy take you, add 'Woof!' This is in the fine tradition of men never really growing up and enjoying playground activity well into their adulthood. It's even more fun if you're in fancy dress and carrying a large inflatable stick of celery.

Sadly the origins of the original 'Ten Men' are unknown. Like so many traditional songs and nursery rhymes, the music and lyrics are both listed as written by 'anon/traditional'. If that's your name, get in touch with the music royalties authorities. You'll be minted.

The signature song of Chelsea is supposed to be 'Blue Is the Colour', and some fans argue it still is. It is played at each home game, but so is the Ska classic 'The Liquidator'. 'Blue Is the Colour' was a single recorded in 1972 and sung by the team, which included Chelsea legends such as Alan Hudson, Peter Osgood and Charlie Cook. Despite this, it still reached number five in the charts. It is still a standard at Stamford Bridge, but such is the popularity of 'Ten Men Went to Mow' that it's debatable which one is now 'the' Chelsea song.

'Blue Is the Colour' will live on, and not just in London. Somewhere, even now, a man in his fifties in a small village in the Czech Republic is humming the song and possibly even singing 'Zelená je tráva, fotbal to je hra' which translates to 'Green is the grass, football is the game'. And then continues:

And that round ball
Is a tricky thing
So each and every one of us
Take care of it
And on the ground pass it on nicely.

This was the Czechoslovak football team's anthem for the 1976 European Championship finals. I think something got lost in translation, perhaps the bit about blue being the colour. No matter, Czechoslovakia went on to the win the tournament.

* * *

From one Blue to another – 'Blue Moon'. This, according to an internet search, is not only a 'prestigious and exciting' Indian restaurant in Aberdeen, it is also a classic pop song and the Manchester City signature tune.

The song is about a blue moon, which is one we see only very rarely. When City fans first took it on, this was very fitting, as for long periods of time they only won games once in a blue moon, and only won trophies once in a month of Sundays – which explains the old Manchester United chant of 'Thirty-two years – fuck all'. Happily for City fans, this has now changed.

The tune of the song 'Blue Moon' dates back to 1933, and the words to the 1934 movie *Manhattan Melodrama*. It has been covered by many different singers, including Frank Sinatra, Elvis Presley, Jan and Dean, Sam Cooke and Doris Day. Most of us probably know it from the Marcels' version. That's the one from 1961 which begins 'Bom-ma-bom, a-bom-bom-a-bom, ba-ba-bom-bom-a-bomp, b-dang-a-dang-dang, b-ding-a-dong-ding Blue Moon'. As a lyric that takes some bettering, especially when mixed in with the 'do wops' 'de doops' and 'wow wow wow wows'. What's not to like? It was a number one hit in both the USA and the UK, and Mars.

There's an extra verse included on the Rod Stewart cover, lamenting the bitter life of a very sad man. Several unsuccessful City managers, from Billy McNeill in 1983 through to Alan Ball, Phil Neal, Stuart Pearce, Sven-Göran Eriksson to Mark Hughes in 2009, may well have reflected on this line. Roberto Mancini broke this possible trend and also taught a generation of young Englishmen how to wear a scarf in a metropolitan metrosexual Man City manner.

'Blue Moon' has also featured in at least seven films, including

Grease, An American Werewolf in London (Sam Cooke's version), and the Jim Jarmusch classic from 1989 – *Mystery Train*. I may be wrong, but I'm not convinced that Jim Jarmusch had much influence on the City fans who, according to Gary James, took up the song at about the same time as the film was released. Mr James doesn't just go to City games, he records everything about them. As the author of *Manchester: A Football History*, he's a proper football historian, and his story, recounted on the MCFC website, is the most reliable account of how *Manhattan Melodrama* became Maine Road dramatics:

> 'The first time I can ever recall it being sung was at the opening game of the 1989–90 season at Liverpool,' he said. 'It had never been sung by fans during the seasons before that.
>
> 'At Anfield, City fans were kept behind for a while after the match and a few lads started singing it as we started to make our way out. They sang a sort of melancholic version, but it caught on.
>
> 'At that time I was doing research for various bits of writing, and recognised that this was unusual – there were plenty of other chants or songs that could have been sung instead [. . .]'
>
> 'People have talked about this to me over the years and most of us share the same memory,' he commented. 'Only a few lads were singing it as we came out – two appeared to be singing it to each other, which was quite funny . . . I don't know the names of the lads who first sang it at Anfield, but I do know they were regulars. I used to see them at away games.'

Apart from the lyrics, there's nothing melancholic about the way the City fans belt it out at the City of Manchester Stadium, sometimes spurred on by versions played over the PA system, including one by the Doves. It is without doubt their signature tune; they own it, and so, if the story that Crewe Alexandra had it first is true, then apologies to the Railway Men – but it's City's now.

They've clearly got a blue thing going on at Man City. There's rip rousing version of 'Singing the Blues' changed to –

I never felt more like singing the blues
City win – United lose
Oh City
You've got me singing the blues.

Crewe Alexandra fans do indeed claim they were first to sing the classic, with their chant 'Blue Moon is an Alex song'. In the same vein, Swansea City may have first dibs on 'I'm Forever Blowing Bubbles', but name the song, ask which club it is associated with, and the answer to 'Blue Moon' will be Manchester City, and to 'Bubbles' it will be West Ham United.

I like 'Bubbles'. It's almost become a good old East End traditional song, despite, as with so many other terrace favourites, originating in America. The song made its debut in a 1919 Broadway musical called *The Passing Show of 1918*. You can find the original tune on YouTube by searching under 'Ben Selvin's Novelty Orchestra I'm Forever Blowing Bubbles' or, for a version with the words, try 'Burr & Campbell – I'm Forever Blowing Bubbles'. Very sweet both are, too. The music is by John Kellette and the words by three different songwriters, James Kendis, James Brockman, and Nat Vincent. For brevity's sake they just put down Jaan Kenbrovin as the author. It's a great terrace anthem; the history is textured and rich. When 40,000 West Ham fans sang it at Wembley in the 2012 play-off final it was inspiring and helped push the team to get back into the Premier League.

Forty thousand sang it, and a few hundred of them followed up at the next opportunity by going to White Hart Lane and singing the Auschwitz song. What those people might be interested to know is that at least one of the men who wrote what is now part of East End and West Ham culture was Jewish. James Brockman, who died in California in 1967, was born Jacob Brachman in Russia in 1886, but left for the United States as a young boy. No Brachman – no 'Bubbles'.

Swansea City's version of how it came to British football is that their fans were singing it in the 1920s, when they played West Ham in an FA Cup tie, and the cheeky cockneys half-inched it! Whatever the truth, by the late 1920s it was staple fare at the Boleyn Ground (Upton Park to you and me). It became so much part of the culture of the day that it was also sung at East End weddings, indeed any family gathering, and sometimes still is. And why not, eh? It's a grand old song.

The origins of why West Ham are known as The Irons and The Hammers are easy to find. WHFC was forged from Thames Iron Works FC, a local company. Tracing how 'Bubbles' got into their bloodstream is more difficult. Much of Britain knew the words in the first half of the twentieth century. The music-hall song had travelled across the Atlantic, featuring in a Jimmy Cagney gangster movie in 1931 called *The Public Enemy*, and the great Harpo Marx from the Marx Brothers enjoyed playing it on a clarinet that blew soap bubbles.

In the 1970s, West Ham's club historian and programme

editor, John Helliar, researched the song and came to the conclusion that it had not, as popular legend has it, been sung at the
West Ham v. Bolton Wanderers FA Cup final in 1923. That was
the famous 'White Horse' final before the days of crowd control,
when most fans mostly controlled themselves.

This is his version of history: in the mid 1920s, schoolboy
football was extremely popular in the West Ham area, with crowds
of up to 1,000 people watching games for the under-fourteen
teams. Helliar says, 'One of the West Ham Champions was Park
School – situated in Ham Park Road [. . .] Its headmaster was a Mr
Cornelius Beal, who was a great football enthusiast, and a friend
of the then West Ham United trainer and subsequent Manager –
Charlie Paynter.' Mr Helliar goes on to explain that Headmaster
Beal used to make up new words to the 'Bubbles' tune. One young
player was nicknamed W. (Billy) J. 'Bubbles' Murray, due to his
resemblance to the boy in the famous painting by Millais entitled
'Bubbles', which was used to advertise Pears Soap. He went on
to play in the West Ham FC boys' team, which attracted a crowd
of 30,000 to the Boleyn Ground for an English schoolboys' final
against Liverpool.

Helliar concludes that, with the song being known through
music-halls, Mr Beal's ditties attaching it to West Ham schoolboy
football, and then 'Bubbles' playing for the club, albeit at a junior
level, the song and the club became synonymous. Further proof
is offered by the historian in a letter he found to Beckton Gas
Works 'Pensioners' Bulletin in 1983. An elderly fan recalled that,
for a period of time (around the 1920s to 1930s, presumably), the
Company Band 'were engaged by the West Ham United Football
Club to play for 20 minutes before the kick-off and 10 minutes at
the interval'. He added: 'We played "Bubbles" and it very quickly

became a favourite with the crowd. If we did not play "Bubbles", the crowd would sing it – so we always played it just before the kick-off.'

The Swansea angle has wings, though. Swansea FC's historian David Farmer has found a newspaper report of the Swansea v. Bury game of January 1921, which says 'At 2.20 p.m. came the ever popular singing of "Bubbles" from the main bank with one tremendous sway'. That's pretty convincing, but either way, Swansea no longer sing it and West Ham do.

More recently, the West Ham FA Cup Final squad of 1975 recorded it, the Cockney Rejects covered the song in 1980 with a punk rock version, happily true to the terrace version, and the song features in the British film *Green Street*. If Swansea want it back, assuming they started it, they'll need to beat the world record for blowing bubbles for a minute, which was set by 23,680 West Ham fans in 1999 before a home game.

'Bubbles' is a great example of community singing and the feeling of belonging it brings. It might well be American in origin, but it's East End now, including the East End of memory for the fans who pour into Upton Park from the commuter towns of Essex of a Saturday.

* * *

The Leeds United anthem differs from most signature tunes for being, at four decades old, relatively modern, with the music and words having been written exclusively for the club. 'Leeds! Leeds! Leeds!' is the title, but it's known as 'Marching on Together'. It is played just before the start of every home game at Elland Road, and the entire stadium joins in. Recently the guy in charge of the PA system has timed it to almost finish just as the referee blows the whistle. He then turns off the speakers and the crowd finish off the song, which is only right and proper and often the best bit of the afternoon before the team goes two–nil down.

It is a tale of love and devotion – 'We're gonna stay with you forever. At least until the world stops turning round.' It acknowledges the sacrifices to be made, 'Everywhere, we're gonna be there', while sensibly leaving out the bit which could have been written 'except for Plymouth away on a wet Tuesday night when the season's almost over and there's not much to play for really'. Then, in one line, it remembers the cup wins, the relegations, the league titles, the bans and Ken Bates – 'And we've had our ups and downs – ups and downs!'

Here we go with Leeds United,
We're gonna give the boys a hand,
Stand up and sing for Leeds United,
They are the greatest in the land

na na na
Everyday, we're all gonna say,
We love you Leeds! Leeds! Leeds!
Everywhere, we're gonna be there,
We love you Leeds! Leeds! Leeds!

Marching on together!
We're gonna see you win
na na na na na na
We are so proud,
We shout it out loud
We love you Leeds! Leeds! Leeds!

We've been through it all together,
And we've had our ups and downs (ups and downs!)
We're gonna stay with you forever,
At least until the world stops going round
Everyday, we're all gonna say
We love you Leeds! Leeds! Leeds!
Everywhere, we're gonna be there,
We love you Leeds! Leeds! Leeds!

Marching on together!
We're gonna see you win
na na na na na na
We are so proud,
We shout it out loud
We love you Leeds! Leeds! Leeds!
We are so proud,
We shout it out loud,
We love you Leeds! Leeds! Leeds!

It was written for the Leeds United team by Barry Mason and Les Reed in 1972, ahead of the Centenary FA Cup Final against Arsenal, which Leeds won one–nil with a second half goal by Alan Clarke. In case you missed it, Charlie George was dispossessed in his own half by Jackie Charlton. He gave the ball to Paul Madeley, who threaded it through to Peter Lorimer, who fed Mick Jones on the wing, who crossed for Clarke to score with a diving header, all accompanied by David Coleman's commentary 'Jones – Clarke – One nil!' But I digress . . . and to digress further, Paul Madeley (who played for England) also ran a decorating business and once came round to measure up our kitchen. Agreed, things were different back then, but now it would be the rough equivalent of Leighton Baines coming round to measure up for the central heating.

When I was a teenager, a period which didn't involve reading newspapers very much, I'd always assumed the 'Leeds! Leeds! Leeds!' song was knocked out in an afternoon by a couple of back-room staff at Elland Road, perhaps working in the ticket office, because, as we've just seen, it was different back then. But no! I couldn't have been more wrong. 'Leeds! Leeds! Leeds!' – and we need to concentrate now – 'Leeds! Leeds! Leeds!' was written by the same men who wrote 'Delilah' and 'It's Not Unusual' for Tom Jones! No, really.

More of Delilah presently, but first the glamorous poptastic swinging '70s Leeds hit written by Mason and Reed. The Leeds website 'The Beaten Generation' revealed all in an article in 2012:

'I recently chatted to sock-tag-inventing artist Paul Trevillion for *The Square Ball* magazine [. . .] Trevillion takes up the tale. "I said to Don, 'We'll have to get a song. Is there anybody you'd like to sing it?' He replied, 'Yes, Tom Jones.' I said, 'We won't get Tom Jones!'" The website then recounts how Trevillion found Les Reed's address, went round, knocked on the door, waited five hours before eventually being invited in, and then persuaded Reed that the great Don Revie did indeed want him to write a song for Leeds.

He said 'I'll get Barry over.' Barry Mason arrived and asked, 'How do you want it?' 'There's a number in Robin Hood with Errol Flynn,' I told him. 'It won an Oscar, it's the greatest music I've ever heard. Can we have it like that?' And Barry started banging on the table, saying

'How about: Here we go with Leeds United! We love you Leeds! Leeds! Leeds!' I said, 'Get the beat from Robin Hood, get that sound!' and they were on for it.

'Leeds! Leeds! Leeds!' was actually the B side of the single, but easily outshone the A side, which was entitled simply 'Leeds United'. It reached number ten in the UK and forty-one in the Irish charts, which is testimony to Leeds being one of those clubs the Irish choose to support, along with Liverpool, Man Utd, and, if pushed, Chelsea, as well as Cork City, Limerick, Shamrock Rovers, Sligo Rovers, and the great Drogheda United, who play at United Park, capacity 2,000.

The club also recorded another song to the tune of 'John Brown's Body', which featured the memorable verse 'Now little Billy Bremner was the captain of the crew, for the sake of Leeds United he would break himself in two'. This always seemed a tad over-enthusiastic to me, but I suppose that is why the late Leeds and Scotland captain ended up such a legend and I ended up in hospital in my late teens after pulling out of a fifty-fifty tackle and getting badly hurt as a result. I still feel a bit of a fraud when shouting 'Get stuck in' at players. You couldn't argue with the second stanza, though: 'His hair was red and fuzzy, he was always black and blue, as Leeds go marching on'.

Leeds also have a song that simply goes 'We are Leeds, We are Leeds, We are Leeds', and then repeats for several minutes until people either get bored or forget the words.

The song 'Leeds! Leeds! Leeds!' is also unusual for being one of the few to cross the Atlantic westwards. In 2012, fans of Major League baseball team the Minnesota Twins took up the song, changing the words to 'Twins! Twins! Twins!' For that, thank, or blame,

Twins fan Andy Sturdevant, who saw the film *The Damned United* about the Don Revie and then short-lived Brian Clough eras. He was so taken by the song that he rewrote it, got together an internet crowd, and set it in motion at the Twins stadium.

Some Leeds fans have welcomed the spreading of the Gospel According to Don Revie. Others think this is a terrible thing, and it's true the American version lacks a certain something (a Yorkshire accent, perhaps?), but hey – imitation: sincerest form of flattery – good luck to them. I think they should invite Leeds fans over for an all-expenses holiday to say thank you.

* * *

Speaking of twins, FC United of Manchester are not, and we need to be absolutely clear here, are *not* the twin brother of Manchester United FC, the club born out of Newton Heath FC in 1902. Proof of this comes from their signature song, possibly the most recent to be written, but one they hope will one day be up there with 'Blue Moon' and 'Forever Blowing Bubbles'. FC United was set up in protest against the takeover of Manchester United by an American multi-millionaire called Malcolm Glazer, who bought the club in May 2005. However, the FC United website says that was not the sole reason:

> The material theft of a Manchester institution, forcibly taken from the people of Manchester, was the tip of a pyramid of destruction, with changing kick off times for the benefit of television, soulless all-seater stadia full of "new" supporters intent to sit back and watch rather than partake in the occasion, heavy handed stewarding and ridiculously priced tickets propping it all up.

In that statement you can hear echoes of Manchester's history of protest. From the Peterloo Massacre, to the Trades Union movement, to the suffragettes, Manchester has been associated with the spirit of 'We're as mad as hell and we're not going to take it any more'.

Shortly after the Glazer takeover, a group of Man Utd supporters created a new, member-owned, not for profit, semi-professional 'punk football' club, which, two weeks after being formed, played a friendly at Leigh in front of 2,552 people. AFC Wimbledon gave them some support, and a ground share was agreed with local giants Bury FC in order to play in division two of the North West Counties Football League. They only went and won the title in their first season, with the final game attracting 6,023 fans! Onwards and upwards. Now mixing it with legends such as Bradford Park Avenue, Kendal, North Ferriby United and Guisely, they played on in the UniBond Premier Division, the Northern Premier League and the Evo-Stik Premier Division.

The spirit of grassroots community activism is written into the DNA of the collective. FC United has tried, partially successfully, to reach out to like-minded organisations, and holds charity initiatives such as The Big Coat Day, where fans collect tonnes of clothes for needy people across the city. Some fans worry that the club's principles are holding them back. They eschew shirt sponsorship, which would help bring in the sort of revenues that would get them into a higher league. So far, they want to do it their way.

There is a legacy of bitterness between some supporters of FC United and Manchester United, but divorces are rarely anything but messy. There are FC United fans who are still de facto supporters of Man Utd, but a lot have made a complete break. All FC United staff are volunteers. I asked one how he would feel if they ever get to the Third Round of the FA Cup and were drawn against Manchester United. He replied, 'I'll be honest with you, it sounds like a dream, but a lot of us hope it will never happen; it would be too painful.'

Sadly, FC United fans have also been involved in minor outbreaks of hooliganism at away games. There's an element of local youth wanting to take on the biggest small boys who come visiting, but there's also a few of the visitors who mistake 'punk football' for 'thug football'. A few FC United fans spend some of their time on the terraces singing anti Leeds, Liverpool and Man City songs. One fan who doesn't join in says, 'They should get over themselves. It's not about that any more, it's about putting the club in the position, not too long from now, of getting league status and getting our own ground.' At time of writing, FC United were moving into a new £5 million, 5,000 capacity stadium in the Manchester district of Moston. By coincidence, Moston is eight miles from Bury and eight miles from Old Trafford, so fans are making a new home equidistant from their two previous abodes.

FC United fans sing a version of the 1949 Ewan MacColl ballad 'Dirty Old Town'. A lot of people think of it as an Irish song, given that The Dubliners and The Pogues have had hits with it. In fact, it's written about Salford, the city where MacColl grew up. FC United fans have changed the words, but not the somewhat melancholy tone, and the 'We may never go home' line bites hard.

We'll build a ground, at Ten Acres Lane,
We'll build a pitch by the old canal,
We'll live the dream down in Newton Heath
We're gonna build our own ground, We're gonna build
* our own ground*

This is our club, belongs to you and me
We're United! United FC!
We may never go home, but we'll never feel down
When we get our own ground, When we get our own ground.

FC United do have a sort of signature song, but it's mostly played in pubs and at charity gigs. It hasn't really taken off on the terraces, but the words, sung to Van Morrison's 'Brown Eyed Girl', tell you where they're coming from and where they hope they're going.

Now where do we go, 3 o'clock on a Saturday,
We go down to Gigg Lane, watch FC United play,
There lots of singing and laughter, young and old all
*   join in too,*
Bring on United, sing the crowd, the team runs out and
*   what a view they see,*
The Bar Scarves twirl,
Yes they see the Bar Scarves twirl
Were playing Punk Football, the way that football used
*   to be.*
The Club belongs to us all, not to a gnome or a PLC
We play in the North West Counties, Blackpool is our
*   Euro Away,*
It'll only cost a couple of quid, to come and watch the
*   FC play and see*
The Bar Scarves twirl
And see those, bar scarves twirl.
And then the crowd all cheer and then they sing,
Sha la la la la la la la la la la la la te da – FC United
The revolution has begun, we are making History,

For 90 minutes the crowd roar, cheering us on to victory
Andy Walsh, Karl Marginson, Luc Zentar and Russell
   Delaney
We want to thank you, for giving us the chance to see
Those Bar Scarves twirl
To see those Bar Scarves twirl
And then the crowd all cheer and then they sing,
Sha la la la la la la la la la la la la te da FC United.

Most people I know in the game wish them well.

*   *   *

At last – we get to the song that has absolutely nothing to do with football, and yet the chorus was tailor made, fitted, booted and suited and ready for the terraces the moment it was written. That song is 'Delilah', but the question to Stoke City is: Why, why, why? Leave to one side the subject matter – he's holding a knife, and her laughter stops – nasty business. This is a song that lends itself to communal singing and bonds together those engaging in it. It's got nothing to do with the Potteries, or Stoke, other than now it's their song.

But again, 'Why?'

The Tom Jones hit was recorded in 1968 and reached number two in the charts. Legend has it that in the late '70s, the old rock group The Sensational Alex Harvey Band played a gig on a Friday night at Stoke's former stadium, the Victoria Ground. The group had got to number seven with a 1975 version of 'Delilah'. You can still find it online from an *Old Grey Whistle Test* recording, which I thoroughly recommend, as it manages to be simultaneously camp, macabre, incredibly '70s, and yet strangely not that dated.

Anyway, it is said the group played the hit at the Victoria Ground and that a lot of Stoke City fans had been in the audience. The next day the team was playing a home game, a group of fans re-lived their experiences of the night before, and it caught on. Another version of events is that Stoke were away at Derby and fans were singing in the pub. The police asked them not to sing songs with swear words, 'Delilah' came on the juke box, and that was that. I'm inclined to believe the first story. Not only is it a better yarn, but, although you can't rule out the Derby police asking fans not to swear, it seems doubtful. Usually the police are content for fans to sing what they want as long as they don't start any trouble.

If you go on Stoke City fan websites you get lots of different versions of when the song first came in, along with variations of the old Tom Jones joke. Well, it's not unusual.

The lyrics have slightly changed over the years, and the Stoke fans applaud each other for their singing when they finish, which is a bit naff, but it's a brilliant song for singing on the train, in the pub, on the terraces, under the stand at half time, in the pub afterwards, and again on the train home. Why? Because they can.

You can easily follow the logic of the 'Delilah' song reaching the terraces – UK hit, anthemic, relatively modern – but Sheffield Wednesday's 'Honolulu Wednesday' is surreal and beyond logic. It's one of the least likely songs ever to be sung by thousands of partially bevvied-up Yorkshiremen, standing in the rain on a cold Saturday afternoon in February in the Steel City.

Oh Honolulu Wednesday
Where did you get those eyes?
Honolulu Wednesday,
In paradise.

Do what? The original is 'Honolulu Baby', from the classic Laurel and Hardy film *Sons of the Desert*. It's their best film by a mile and they squeeze every bit of desperately sad, desperately funny comedy out of sixty-eight minutes. As members of a fraternity, the hapless duo have to swear a sacred oath that they will attend a convention in Chicago. They then tell a pack of lies to their wives in order to get there. The lies are 'too far fetched not to be true'. Halfway through comes a dance scene in a nightclub and the song 'Honolulu Baby'. Towards the end it appears again, this time sung by Oliver Hardy, armed only with a bowler hat and a ukulele. But the film is from 1933 – it's not like it's the *The Sound of Music*, or *Mary Poppins*, whose songs are vaguely part of the soundtrack to our lives. However, someone, somewhere was as taken by the film and the song, as were previous generations, which is another fine mess Wednesday fans have got themselves into.

The Wednesday online site www.sheffwed.vitalfootball has various fans' memories of when it was taken up. One says that it was on the way to a Norwich away game – '"Honolulu baby, where did you get that smile" was sung to the passing girlies on the way to the ground. Then it changed to Honolulu Wednesday on the return trip (when we had won).' I prefer the following version of events, but I have my doubts about it:

First time I remember it was drinking on the high street near Palace's ground on the last away game of 91/92. It was the game when Mark Bright scored at the end to put paid to our hopes of going in to the last game of the season with chance of winning the title (L**ds won it). Next to the pub was a grocers with fruit and veg outside. A big lad picked up a pineapple and put it on his head whilst singing Honolulu Baby. There quickly built a chorus of Honolulu Wednesday.

The story sounds about right, and you can picture it, but many older Wednesday fans are sure the song was already a standard by the late 1980s. However, one says, 'I think Stan Laurel started it on the Kop one game when it went a bit quiet. Ollie couldn't make it that day [as] he was out moving a piano.'

What would Stanley have made of all this? Well, he was born in Argyle Street, Ulverston, then Lancashire, now Cumbria, in 1890, so it's unlikely that, had he stayed in England, he would have been a fan of a Yorkshire club. Nevertheless, this hybrid of English terrace humour and the American silver screen is a roundabout, surreal, but fitting tribute to one of the biggest (and funniest) Hollywood stars Britain has ever produced.

Just up the road, or should I say 'just up road', is another proud Yorkshire football club with a fine past, a middling present, an uncertain future, and a song which acknowledges all three realities. Huddersfield won the Division One championship on three consecutive seasons in the 1920s. Since then, it's been mostly downhill; which explains the more recent song:

Won it three times
We've won it three times
We've won it three times
None of us remember but
We've won it three times.

Huddersfield Town also have an official song which is in the spirit of 'On the Ball, City!' but it doesn't appear to have worn so well.

There's a team that is dear to its followers
Their colours are bright blue & white,
They're a team of renown, the pride of the Town,
And the game of Football is their delight.
All the while, upon the field of play,
Thousands loudly cheer them on their way.
Often you can hear them say, who can beat the Town today?
Then the bells will ring so merrily
Every goal, shall be a memory
So Town play up, and bring the Cup
Back to Huddersfield.

In the 'play up' line you can almost hear the ghosts of thousands of young boys who swung their rattles around in the old Leeds Road stadium in the 1920s. These days, the new John Smith's stadium still resounds to the traditional song but less so than to the faintly surreal tinge, which so many modern songs have, of a homage to the giant TV mast up above the town on Emley Moor.

This is Huddersfield's answer to the *Angel of the North*. It may lack some of the artistic merit of the *Angel*, but it has three things going for it. It was built before the *Angel*, it is ten times taller than the Angel, and, unlike the *Angel*, it can transmit television pictures! Eat your heart out, *Angel* eyes. No wonder it's celebrated on the terraces.

Oh Emley Moor
Has got a mast
Oh Emley Moor has got a mast
It's bigger than the Eiffel tower
Emley Moor has got a mast.

These are self-evident truths. Emley Moor does indeed have a mast, and at 330.4 metres it is indeed taller than the Eiffel Tower's 324 metres. It now has a Grade II listing preservation order on it, as well as a lift and a viewing platform. From its heights the views are marvellous, and, unless it's foggy, you can see a lot of sheep.

It may be surreal to hymn praise to a TV mast. Actually, now I think of it, no, maybe it's not; in fact it makes sense. However, what is surreal is how a folksong about love and suicide, made famous by a man born some time around 1888 on a plantation in the Deep South of the United States, is being sung on the terraces at Bristol Rovers FC in the twenty-first century. 'Goodnight Irene' is the song and Huddie William Ledbetter is the singer. He's better known as Lead Belly and was a rough, tough, hard-drinking jailbird from Louisiana. He could also hold a tune.

Lead Belly did time on at least three occasions, the first in 1918 for killing a man in a row over a woman. In 1930, while serving a sentence for attempted murder, he was heard singing by a musicologist called John Lomax, who began recording Lead Belly's songs and his twelve-string guitar. His repertoire included an old number he said he'd learned from his uncle in the previous century – 'Goodnight Irene'. It's an example of late nineteenth-century black American country blues. The lyrics reflect the hardships of the times and Lead Belly's own gambling problems; and, improbably, it has given the British a catchphrase, and a song that is a favourite in the blue half of the English city of Bristol. Lead Belly died in New York in 1949. He is buried in his native Louisiana.

I asked your mother for you
She told me that you was too young

"Dirty Northern Bastards!"

I wish to the Lord I'd never seen your face
Or heard your lying tongue.
Irene goodnight, Irene goodnight
Goodnight Irene, Goodnight Irene
I'll see you in my dreams.

Sometimes I live in the country
Sometimes I live in the town
Sometimes I have a great notion
To jump into the river and drown
Irene goodnight, Irene goodnight
Goodnight Irene, Goodnight Irene
I'll see you in my dreams.

Stop ramblin', stop your gamblin'
Stop stayin' out late at night
Go home to your wife and your family
Sit down by the fireside bright
Irene goodnight, Irene goodnight
Goodnight Irene, Goodnight Irene
I'll see you in my dreams.

I love Irene God knows I do
Love her till the sea run dry
And if Irene turns her back on me
I'm gonna take morphine and die
Irene goodnight, Irene goodnight
Goodnight Irene, Goodnight Irene
I'll see you in my dreams.

'Goodnight Irene' is now a catchphrase meaning 'It's all over', or 'And that was that'. Sadly, it is falling out of use. The lyric 'Sometimes I have a great notion' inspired Ken Kesey's novel *Sometimes a Great Notion*, and the whole thing inspired the group Nirvana. Kurt Cobain was a huge admirer. He took another of Lead Belly's songs, 'Where Did You Sleep Last Night?' in a new direction, but, alas, took the lyrics to 'Goodnight Irene' to a tragic conclusion.

'Goodnight Irene' crossed the Atlantic in the 1940s, after Pete Seeger released a cover that went to number one in the USA and was played over here. A Frank Sinatra cover then made number one in the UK in 1950. After that it was covered by a variety of singers, including Lonnie Donegan, Brian Wilson and Bryan Ferry. So, by the early 1950s it would have been well known in the West Country and would have had a fair bit of radio play. How and why it was adopted by Rovers is another matter. There are several plausible and possibly related theories.

The old Eastville stadium sat alongside the River Frome and so was a convenient place to have a great notion and 'jump in the river and drown' after yet another home defeat. Another says that Rovers were playing Plymouth Argyle off the park in a game in the early 1950s and as the Argyle supporters began to drift out, the home fans broke out into 'Goodnight Argyle'. It's plausible, although there wasn't as much singing in those days and there were fewer travelling fans. Either way, it stuck, and has become the official club anthem. Some Bristol City fans heap scorn on the 'Gasheads', as Rovers are known, for singing what is now an obscure song entirely unrelated to football. I think it's in the gloriously barking mad surreal spirit of the best of British.

* * *

Bristol Rovers have among the most unlikely songs to make it to the terraces, but Derby County have connections with probably the oldest. Its origins possibly go back as far as Roman Britain. However, the song goes on, and on, and 'On! On! On!' and has never really taken off on the terraces. Instead 'The Ballad of the Derby Ram' remains a folksong, some of which is sung by Derby fans in the pub, but 'Steve Bloomer's Watching' is probably the signature song of the club.

'The Ballad of the Derby Ram' is an old 'boasting song', which cheerfully admits to lying, and tells the tall tale of a giant ram on its way to be butchered in Derby on market day. It was the biggest ram 'that was ever fed on hay [...] every foot that he set down, it covered an acre of land'.

> *And indeed me lads, 'tis true me lads*
> *For I never was known to lie*
> *And if you'd have been in Derby*
> *You'd have seen him as well as I.*

(Then it all goes a bit Tarantino . . .)

> *The man who killed this ram, sir*
> *Was drowned in the blood*
> *And the little boy that held the bowl*
> *Was washed away in the flood . . .*

> *And all the boys in Derby*
> *Came begging for his eyes*
> *To kick them round the market place*
> *'Cos they were football size . . .*

Thank goodness for Tesco and cling-wrap, eh? The song ends with what sounds to me like threats with menaces – 'I've nothing more to say, but give us more ale and we'll all of us go away'. As it says in Ecclesiastes, 'There is nothing new under the sun', and in the last line you can hear the connection between the lads in Derby in the sixteenth century and those of today. The song is part of a mummers' play called 'The Derby Tup', which goes back to medieval times and was sometimes performed by men who went house to house, hence the 'give us some beer and we'll leave' sentiment.

At one point in the play the ram's horns are gilded, a practice that can be traced back to Roman times. The words of the (relatively) modern song date to at least the 1860s, but there is reference to it existing in the sixteenth century. Variations of the song are still to be heard in Australia and the USA, and in the latter it was also turned into a New Orleans jazz standard called 'Didn't He Ramble?'

Derby takes its sheep very seriously. There are two statues of said ram in the town; the song was the regimental song of the Derbyshire Militia in 1855, and of the 95th Derbyshire Regiment, and it remains associated with the football club that has the ram as its emblem and nickname. However, it is not the official anthem, according to club historian Colin Gibson, who says that that honour is conferred upon 'Steve Bloomer's Watching', which has a rather shorter and less bloody history. Written in 1997, it is a rewrite of an Aussie Rules football song which was taken up by two Derby County fans who heard it 'down under'. Club officials heard about it in the local Derbyshire media and took it up as a professional project. The actor and County fan Robert Lindsay was drafted in to help sing it, along with several players and the then manager Jim Smith. It was released under the name 'Robert Lindsay and the Pride Park Posse'.

On Boxing Day 1997, Derby were at home to Newcastle United, and as the teams ran out, the song was blasted out over the PA system. It was then played at every home game until the end of the season and caught on with the fans. And who is Steve Bloomer, I hear anyone not from Derby ask? Steve Bloomer is that bloke immortalised in bronze who stands next to the home dugout at the Pride Park stadium. He was the Derby and England striker in the 1890s and, apart from an abject failure to bite people, was on a par, if not better, with Luis Suárez as a goal-scoring machine. He scored 240 goals in 376 games for County, and 28 goals in 23 games for country.

The Bloomer song, the statue and the Derby Ram are all examples of how a club is embedded into a town's consciousness and can help foster community spirit.

Our history's full of legends,
And football played on high,
Raich Carter, Peter Doherty,
You should have seen 'em fly.
Now we all just love football,
But will we lift the crown,
The noise goes up, the Rams come out,
Onto the hallowed ground.

Steve Bloomer's Watching,
Helping them fight,
Guiding our heroes,
In the black and the white.
All teams who come here,
There's nowhere to hide,

Everyone is frightened,
Of that Derby pride.

The fans finish this off with a rousing chant of 'Derby! Derby!' The only Derby County-supporting friend I have does not have mixed feelings about this song. No, he's very clear, telling me: 'Personally? Me? I hate it!' But that is a minority opinion and you tinker with tradition at your peril. You also manufacture it at your peril, as stories from Everton and Aston Villa make clear.

First Everton. If you are of a certain age, have been to Goodison Park, or have been paying attention when they are on TV, you will have noticed that the Toffees run out to the theme from *Z Cars*, the TV police series that ran for several decades in the Middle Ages. I say run out, and they used to run out, like every other team, whenever they wanted. As long as all twenty-two of them were there when the referee blew his whistle, they could come out whenever they wanted. It was always quite fascinating to see which team would come out first. I was going to say 'all twenty-two were there for 3 o'clock', but that's gone as well. As it happens, I am not someone who believes nostalgia isn't what it used to be, for two reasons. One, in those days we had to get up, walk across the room, and press a button to change the TV channel, and two – there was no t'interweb thingy and I like the t'interweb thingy. Eeeh, it were hard back then.

Anyway, if you're under forty and missed it, *Z Cars* revolutionised Brit cop shows. It was a leap forward from *Dixon of Dock Green*, a bit like the leap from *Kojak* to *Hill Street Blues*. If you're under thirty I'll try again; it was like the leap from *Hill Street Blues* to *NYPD Blue*. If you're under twenty-five, then neither of us have the faintest idea what the other is talking about, as I gave up watching TV about five years ago and you probably have every episode of 24 in a microchip glued to your frontal lobes.

Anyway, *Z Cars*. It was set in one of the new towns built after the Second World War and, in case anyone missed the point, the writers called it 'Newtown'. Everyone knew that it was based on Kirkby near Liverpool, but the BBC never let on in case local residents wrote to the newspapers and complained. Think of the *Benefits Street* row, then magnify it by several million per cent, because in those far off days there was bugger all to do of an evening except watch telly and there were only three channels.

Newtown was Haard with a capital Haa. It had proper coppers in it wot spoke with regional accents and it knocked the soft southern soap opera from London's *Dock Green* into a flashing blue helmet. The *Dock Green* boys meandered around with their heads going all the way to the top of their helmets, their hands behind their backs and 'Evening all' playing on their lips as they cheerfully ticked off another youngster for scrumping. OK, it wasn't quite like that. Sometimes they said things like 'move along now, nothing to see here'. It was quite a shock when PC George Dixon was shot and injured in one of the TV episodes; mind you, not as bad as when he was shot and killed in the film version. I liked him, we all did, Dixon – not Bogarde, though he was all right as well – but Dixon personified what we wanted life to be like, even though we knew it wasn't. Honestly, it was worse than when Bambi was shot.

Meanwhile, oop north, the *Z Cars* boys sat in Ford Escorts wearing flat-peaked police hats, staring moodily out into the rainy night and preparing to give some to the ne'er-do-wells of Kirby. It was great. So far, so north-west. This was, after all, ten years before Merseyside had been invented. The police even had Lancashire insignia, as Kirby was in the Red Rose county in the 1960s. So why did Everton embrace *Z Cars*?

There's a clue in the name of a pub in Whitefield Drive in the real Kirby. It's called 'The Johnny Todd', and 'Johnny Todd' is a nineteenth-century Liverpool folksong. The pub, in case you're visiting, has a 'well decorated and comfortably furnished bar/lounge' and 'At the rear of the building is a children's play area and a beer garden which is furnished with wooden bench seating'. If I gambled, which I used to but don't any more, I'd wager they have the football on of a Sunday.

So this pub, and more importantly the song after which it is named, is why, the first time the opening music for *Z Cars* came on TV in 1962, half of Liverpool sat up and said, 'Hang on – that's Johnny Todd!' The other 49 per cent were watching ITV, and 1 per cent were tuned to BBC2.

Johnny was a bit of lad, according to the song, and he gets his comeuppance, but I reckon he had a close shave and only narrowly escaped marrying a mad floozy given to weeping and wailing and tearing her hair out.

Johnny Todd he took a notion
For to sail the ocean wide,
And he left his true love behind him,
Weeping by the Liverpool tide.

For a week she wept full sorely,
Tore her hair and wrung her hands,
Then she met another sailor,
Walking on the Liverpool sands.

'O fair maid, why are you weeping
For your Johnny gone to sea?
If you wed with me tomorrow
I will kind and constant be.

'I will buy you sheets and blankets,
I'll buy you a wedding ring,
You shall have a gilded cradle
For to rock your baby in.'

Johnny Todd came back from sailing,
Sailing o'er the ocean wide,
But he found that his fair and false one
Was another sailor's bride.

All young men who go a-sailing
Or to fight the foreign foe,
Don't you leave your love like Johnny,
Marry her before you go.

There's a Scottish version of this song, but in it the fair maid appears far less agitated and hangs about until Johnny Todd shows up again.

Whether or not the thespians playing Newtown's finest in *Z Cars* were aware of all this drama is unknown, but, according to the toffee.web.com site, one of the actors was an Everton fan (PC Sweet) and he invited some of the cast along to see a game. To welcome them, the club officials played the *Z Cars* theme as the team ran out, it caught on, and since 1963 has been a permanent fixture. Well, permanent apart from the unfortunate incident in

1993 when the then Everton chairman, Peter Johnson, decided that tradition wasn't what it used to be and part-exchanged the *Z Cars* theme for 'Fanfare for the Common Man' by the 1970s prog rock supergroup Emerson, Lake and Palmer.

'You what?' said the Gladys Street End. 'Fanfare for the what? Give over, soft lad!' Mr Johnson's name was considered akin to the mud on Neville Southall's boots. He was universally barracked, the 'Fanfare' fell on stony ears, and the chairman was made very aware that you don't mess with *Z Cars* and Everton. A few weeks later, the Everton legend Joe Royle was appointed manager. Mr Johnson wisely decided to turn a deaf ear as the team once again began to run out to the tune that defines the club.

Now that's what I call a proper football story; most of it might even be true. When it comes down to it, the fans decide what is and isn't tradition, because the players and managers come and go, but the fans span the generations.

What is now known as the signature song of Leeds United was the B side of what was supposed to be sung, but the fans decided otherwise. That 'Blue Moon', 'Goodnight Irene', 'Delilah' and 'Honolulu Wednesday' are signature songs is entirely due to the fans embracing a song from far away and making it part of their club's folklore. You can invent tradition; the Derby 'Bloomers' song shows it's possible, but only if the fans buy into the idea.

The misguided attempt to play *Z Cars* off the park at Goodison reminds me of the Aston Villa tale of 'The Bells Are Ringing'. Ding dong! It's not a bad song; in fact it's a really good song, especially when Judy Garland and the sublime Gene Kelly sang it in the 1942 Busby Berkeley film *For Me and My Gal*. When several hundred Aston Villa fans were invited by the club to sing it on the steps in front of the impressive Aston Villa entrance, it was still a good song. It might even have become the club's signature song; but it didn't.

The bells are ringing
for the Claret and Blue.
The fans are singing,
for the Claret and Blue.
Everybody is knowing,
to the Villa they're going,
Where the Villa are showing,
We're the best in the land!

We're congregating
for the Claret and Blue.
The Holte End's waiting
for the Claret and Blue.
Everybody is knowing,
to the Villa they're going.
Where the Villa are showing
We're the best in the land!

The club tried hard with a big advertising push, the fans sang it, and it sounded good, but it didn't really catch on as the signature tune. It is not in the club's DNA, and the fans have voted with their vocal cords that it's probably not going to be.

Some of the worst (songs) do not come from the terraces via popular culture but are manufactured. Many of the England World Cup and Euro campaign songs are examples of that. You can just about forgive skiffle musician Lonnie Donegan for 'World Cup

Willie' in 1966, as it was of its time, when bobble hats and rattles were not a distant memory, and when the spirit of 'Play up and play the game' was still clinging on to British culture. And 1970's effort for the Mexico World Cup was – like the England defence in the West Germany quarter-final game – passable. The hook was 'Back home, they'll be watching and waiting', which captured the idea of our boys going 'over there' to do battle.

Fearing that they might be called to the recording studios again, the England teams conspired not to qualify for the 1974 and 1978 World Cup finals, but at some point they had to man up, so in 1982, Ron Greenwood's England squad strode across the zebra crossing into the famous Abbey Road studios in London and belted out 'This Time (We'll Get It Right)' before going to Spain and getting it wrong. It's possible the players never fully recovered from having to sing that song. Given that it was written by the group Smokie, who gave the world the gift of 'Living Next Door to Alice', this was poor fare.

Remember 'The Whole World at Our Feet' by the England squad from 1986? You're in good company. Nor does anyone else. It entered the charts at number sixty-six, as England went out to Argentina and Maradona's 'Hand of God'.

The 1990 World Cup finals were in Italy and produced a decent official song – 'World in Motion' by Englandneworder, which many fans agree is the best approved effort. Knowing they couldn't better the John Barnes rap in 'World in Motion', the players and manager Graham Taylor conspired not to qualify for the 1994 World Cup in the USA. It was left to Germany to record that tournament's most embarrassing song, called 'Far Away in America' by Village People and Deutsche Fussball-Nationalmannschaft.

Euro 96 had the unofficial 'Three Lions', which caught on, but the official 'We're in this Together' by Simply Red was simply awful and not even on nodding acquaintance with the charts. In 1998, by far the most popular song to be sung over and over again, was the deeply unofficial 'Vindaloo' by Fat Les. Yet again it proved that the terraces make the decisions. The song was originally a parody of the worst football songs, but the fans embraced irony and absurdity and made it their own. The official 'Three Lions 98' was a decent effort and made it to number one in the charts, with 'Vindaloo' number two. Less popular was 'Meat Pie Sausage Roll (Come on England, Gis a Goal)' by Grandad Roberts and His Son Elvis, which charted at number seventy.

Remember 2002? 'We're on the Ball' from Ant and Dec? I thought not.

The 2004 Euro finals threw up a surprise. The FA gave fans a vote on three possible slogans – 'Pride of Lions', 'United England' and 'All Together Now'. The latter was the clear favourite with 59 per cent of the vote, and from there it was an easy connection to The Farm's hit of 1990 of the same name, which was then remixed and re-released. It retained the hook lines, which were based on the descending chord sequence from Pachebel's 'Canon in D Major'.

What is surprising is that the FA didn't just leave the slogan as a standalone but went on to use a song that could be considered political. It is about the famous football match between British and German troops on Christmas Day 1914. The Farm were a band from Liverpool with strong left-wing sentiments and the song was from their first album, *Spartacus*. The lead singer, Peter Hooton, allowed the song to be used on condition that the lyrics weren't changed.

Remember boy that your forefathers died
Lost in millions for a country's pride
But they never mention the trenches of Belgium
When they stopped fighting and they were one
[. . .]
Countries' borders were right out of sight
When they joined together and decided not to fight
[. . .]
The boys had their say they said no
Stop the slaughter and let's go home
Let's go, let's go, let's go, let's go . . .

The Farm were part of the debate about the rights and wrongs of the First World War long before the great debate broke out again on the hundredth anniversary of 1914. There has always been far more ambivalence in the UK about the First World War than the Second.

You won't remember the 2010 World Cup song because the then manager Fabio Capello banned one, saying he 'wanted to be fully focused on the football'. He wasn't. The official 2014 offering, 'Greatest Day', was most memorable for featuring towering pop supremos such as Emma Bunton and Pixie Lott, and for Gary Lineker singing in the key of W flat (minor). Other commercial England football songs are available, but none of them, nor the ones mentioned, define the team or country (except perhaps 'Vindaloo' . . .).

* * *

At club level, though, all the signature songs have something to offer and have become part of how fans identify themselves and bond with each other. Derby's is pure local pride and Norwich has the original spirit of the game. Sheffield Wednesday, Stoke and Bristol Rovers give us the surreal humour of the terraces, Liverpool's 'You'll Never Walk Alone' is theirs, but it's also football's song and belongs to everyone.

My favourite though, by some distance, is Hibernian's 'Sunshine on Leith', from The Proclaimers' album of the same name, released in 1988. Leith is just north of Edinburgh, which is home to Hibs FC and their local rivals, Hearts FC. Leith is at the mouth of the Water of Leith and was the birthplace of twins Charlie and Craig Reid, who make up The Proclaimers. It is an achingly beautiful song. It has a touch of melancholy, as does many a football song, but it also has hope and faith, and, again like many a traditional football song, it refers to a higher spirit that will see us right in the end. In that, it echoes 'Keep Right On to the End of the Road' and, to a lesser extent, 'You'll Never Walk Alone' (but perhaps not so much 'Honolulu Baby' . . .).

If you get a chance, look up the YouTube footage of the celebrations for the Hibernian FC CIS Cup Final win in 2007 (search for 'Hibernian Massed Choir'). At the end the PA plays 'Sunshine on Leith' and the entire Hibernian support joins in, as do many players. Down on the pitch is manager John Collins, who was new to management. His father, Norrie, had died two months earlier and his dying wish was that John would lead Hibs to victory. At one point in the song John looks up to the heavens, and you just know he's thinking of his dad. It's heart-wrenching stuff and it speaks to why we love the game. It has everything to do with 'You'll Never Walk Alone' and nothing to do with throwing coins at Wayne Rooney.

In that moment football is distilled back to the fact that it is a game, a beautiful game, *the* beautiful game. At all levels it's fun; at the highest level it is an amazing display of skill, passion, determination and the triumph of human endeavour. Some people see players cavorting around the pitch and are disdainful. It's worth remembering that winning a trophy is a massive professional achievement, coming after years and years of hard work and, like in any job, is a reflection of that work. John looked up to the sky, remembered his dad and all the help he'd given him and at that moment, 'the Chief put sunshine on Leith'.

My heart was broken, my heart was broken
Sorrow Sorrow Sorrow Sorrow
My heart was broken, my heart was broken

You saw it, You claimed it
You touched it, You saved it

My tears are drying, my tears are drying
Thank you Thank you Thank you Thank you
My tears are drying, my tears are drying

Your beauty and kindness
Made tears clear my blindness

While I'm worth my room on this earth
I will be with you
While the Chief, puts sunshine on Leith
I'll thank Him for His work
And your birth and my birth.

"Dirty Northern Bastards!"

Yeah, yeah, yeah, yeah
My heart was broken, my heart was broken
Sorrow Sorrow Sorrow Sorrow
My heart was broken, my heart was broken
You saw it, You claimed it
You touched it, You saved it

While I'm worth my room on this earth
I will be with you
While the Chief, puts sunshine on Leith
I'll thank Him for His work
And your birth and my birth.

Amen.

Extra Time

'You're 'Avin' a Laugh'

Now, let's get this straight: the father of the splendidly named Dean Gerken is not a cucumber. The cucumber and the gherkin are very different things, as, I'm sure, are Mr Gerken and his son; it is unfair to chant 'Your dad's a cucumber' at Dean. It's also Vegetablist. However, Dean can sometimes be found in a pickle. When such a fate befalls the Colchester and now Ipswich goalkeeper, and he lets more than one shot into the old onion bag, especially in unfortunate circumstances, he may be subjected to the chant: 'Stayed in a burger, you should have stayed in a burger.'

The knowing chuckle that goes round when we hear a really funny, clever chant is part of the communal experience of following football. It's nowhere near as powerful as the communal singing of the signature songs that bring the sense of belonging, history and community, but it's on the same page.

Away days often bring out the best, and sometimes the worst, in football fans. There's a feeling of venturing into strange and foreign lands, such as Coventry, or High Wycombe, or Peterborough, and once there, you have to remind the locals of your inherent superiority and their deficiencies. Any club redeveloping its stadium, and having one side of the pitch open to the uncaring outside world, will be asked, 'Shall we build a stand for you?' If the ground is one of those new ones that looks as if it has been fitted together with brightly painted corrugated iron and bits of Lego, the home fans will be told, 'Your ground's from B&Q'.

When Rotherham United couldn't afford a ground any more, they moved to the Don Valley athletics stadium, which boasts a fine running track. It's perfect for running – you could run 400 metres around that pitch in about 44.9 seconds, and some folk do – but it's rubbish for watching football. If you're standing behind the goal, you need binoculars to see the halfway line. The last time Leeds United fans visited, they broke out into a chorus of 'Here for the shot put. We're only here for the shot put.' Rotherham is a fine community club, and I wish them well. Happily for all, in 2012, Rotherham FC moved into a modern £20 million stadium. I think it was maybe on special offer from Homebase.

In the event of a ground being a little on the cramped side, the cry will go up to the tune of 'Oh When the Saints':

My garden shed – is bigger than this
My garden shed is bigger than this
It's got a door, and a window
My garden shed is bigger than this.

Here special mention must go to Sittingbourne FC of the Isthmian League Division One South. They took the familiar chant and came up with an original version, directed at any passing visiting player they considered dodgy:

> *My niece of two! – is better than you!*
> *My niece of two is better than you.*
> *She's got a doll, and a pushchair.*
> *My niece of two is better than you.*

Geography is always a useful subject for a funny chant. Torquay United's regional pride, for example, was displayed in a song aimed at fans unfortunate enough to come from a landlocked hellhole such as, say, Cheltenham: 'Have you ever seen a beach?' Reading (The Royal) came up with a clever one when visiting Peterborough (The Posh) – 'You're Posh, but you're not Royal'.

Fans visiting Blundell Park, home to Grimsby Town, may wish they had gone to McDo's, rather than the chippy, when greeted with 'We piss on your fish – yes we do'. Grimsby fans have also been heard to chant 'Fish, Fish, Fish!' over and over again. Why? Because they can. They've also been known to go a bit 'Egg chasers', taking the England rugby song but changing it to 'Swing low – sweet halibut'. Fleetwood Town's finest are also known to be fond of a bit of battered fish. To the tune of the Sex Pistols' 'Anarchy in the UK', they go with 'I wanna destroy Southport FC! 'Cos I wanna be, Cod Army'. This is entirely fitting, as the Sex Pistols, and John Lydon in particular, were always in the great British end-of-pier music-hall tradition.

It is especially helpful if you can embrace the inner stereo-type. Many Bristol City fans enjoy playing up the 'Wurzels' image. 'Drink Up Thee Cider' is a favourite song, 'I Am a Cider Drinker' usually gets a run out, and recently they have added two new songs to the straw-hanging-out-of-their-hair repertoire. The first is in honour of Natch Cider – a sort of local brew, if you count Taunton as being near Bristol (thirty-seven miles apart, as you asked). It goes: 'Nana nana nanananannanana – Natch Cider in a can – Cider in a can'. They also hymn praise to Thatchers Gold, which is not what Maggie got for selling off the Crown Jewels, but a fine premium cider from the town of Sandford, North Somerset. This is practically within combine harvester distance from Bristol – a mere thirteen miles. The song for Thatchers Gold is sung on the terraces to the tune of the old Spandau Ballet song –'Thatchers Gold – Gold!' Thatchers, still a family-run business, 110 years into production, appears to have a sense of humour, as in 2007, it produced a cider called 'Wurzel Me'.

You'd also hope the Swiss can grin and bear it and could take Newcastle United's celebratory chant after scoring away in Zurich – 'You're not yodelling, You're not yodelling, You're not yodelling any more'.

Charlton fans suggested that their opposite numbers in Millwall reside in a part of South London that might encourage *Shameless* behaviour:

> *He's coming for you*
> *He's coming for you*
> *Jeremy Kyle*
> *He's coming for you.*

Some chants just fall out of fashion. Few fans now sing the '80s classic 'Oh whay oh whay oh whay oh whay'. You can still hear it, but it's no longer front and centre. Variations on a theme of 'Knees Up Mother Brown' have gone, and the 'You're just a small town in

X' chant is becoming dated, perhaps through overuse. Reading is not a small town in Swindon. West Bromwich is not a small town in Walsall. However, most football fans will agree that Hebden Bridge is small town in Yorkshire, and Stamford Bridge is a small town in Moscow.

If the town that away fans are visiting is deemed particularly scuzzy, they can always console themselves with the song 'You have to live here – we get to go home'. This is far superior to the dreary 'Your town's a shit hole, I want to go home'. Whenever I hear that, I always want to shout 'Well, go on then – no one's stopping you', but there are two things that prevent me from so doing. Firstly, I've always had an aversion to being punched in the face. Secondly, it's always possible that the song may be being performed at Millwall, in which case you can't go home, or at least not yet. The New Den is the Hotel California of British football: you can check it out, but it feels as if you can never leave.

Last time I was there, the guys I go to games with left their car at my house in West London, we took my car down to Westminster, where I know a parking spot that is free on Saturdays, then it's Westminster Tube to London Bridge, and train to Millwall.

So far – so away day. After the game, the police locked us in for forty minutes. That is plenty enough time to reflect on a dull one–one draw and for Millwall fans to go home. Clearly some have mobility issues, because as we emerged, blinking in the new dawning realisation that we weren't going to make the play offs, there were still several hundred of them outside, waiting to say goodbye.

Perhaps this is an old South London custom akin to the Arab culture of hospitality, where you walk as far as you can with your guest before saying farewell. In Millwall's version, you then throw things at the visitors as they depart. No matter. We got to

London Bridge, where some Millwall fans were taking hospitality to extremes and had gathered there for a final farewell – you guys!

I informed an officer of the Metropolitan Police that my car was in Westminster, so I needed to take a different tube line to the one the other away fans would use, to which he replied, 'Fuck off back up north'. The tube train rattled under London, heading for King's Cross without stopping. Station names flashed by in a blur. When we did come to halt, at a station in the centre, I again attempted to negotiate with a member of the constabulary – to no avail. At Euston, I tried once more. This time I made the mistake of calling the officer 'son', to which he replied 'Fuck off to King's Cross, old man', which was a bit rude. I'm not that old. At King's Cross I made another break for freedom, heading out of the station, only to be pushed back with the other fans all the way towards the platform, where the train was waiting to deport everyone up north.

At last reason prevailed and we made it out of the Kafkaesque labyrinth that is Millwall away and headed to the pub. It had been an epic journey, the saga now for ever imprinted on my memory and worthy of being passed down from generation to generation. The problem with that, however, is that neither of my children like football. I frequently tell them they are a great disappointment to me, but as that hasn't changed their minds, oddly, I've had to change my will. Anyway, I console myself with the thought that one day Vic and Bob may write a song about my never-ending journey called – 'Didn't We Have a Lovely Time – The Day We Went to the New Den'.

A much better day out is down on the south coast. Southend United have a good song with which to show one-upmanship if playing any other club from a seaside town. The song bursts with local pride, and uses 'Oh When the Saints' as its template:

Oh Southend pier is longer than yours!
Oh Southend pier is longer than yours!
It's got some shops, and a railway
Oh Southend pier is longer than yours!

This is true. It does have some shops, and a railway. It is a mighty fine pier, visited by millions of Londoners and many a football fan. According to the local council, it is 'The longest pleasure pier in the world'. This is a boast many a testosterone-fuelled visiting male fan might wish to make about parts of their anatomy, but which is true only of Southend-on-Sea's pier. Proof of this is its 1.34 mile Grade II-listed length, but that is changeable, depending on the waves, what decade it is, fires breaking out, and whether passing sea captains are driving their boats erratically.

It was first built because Southend-on-Sea, a perfectly nice coastal town, is actually Southend-on-Mud. The sea being some way further out, near a place called France. Boats don't float on mud, and as the sea was some way off in the distance, they needed a pier, and they got a wooden one in 1830. Alas, it was only 600 feet long and the sea wouldn't even meet it halfway at low tide, so they extended it to three times its length and by 1848 it was the longest pier in Europe. However, the planner hadn't planned on so many people coming to use it and it quickly wore out and had to be replaced with an iron version in 1887. The Pavilion then burnt down in 1958 and was replaced by a bowling alley. This burnt down in 1995. In 2005, the railway station, ice cream shop and sea shell emporium burnt down.

Before this, though, in 1986, the MV *Kingsabbey* crashed into the pier, severing the new pier head and destroying the boathouse. As this book went to print, Southend pier was intact, and was not on fire, but there was a ship worryingly close to it. I mention that because if you draw Southend United in the Cup this year, or your club plays in the same league as the Shrimpers, it's worth a visit, as the pier is only two miles from the stadium, and a mile from the train station. If, however, you have an away day at SUFC in a couple of years' time, they may have moved to a new stadium in 'Fossets Farm' on the outskirts of town. This is not located near Southend pier, but is close to a Waitrose. Only one of these two institutions gets a name check in the *Hitchhiker's Guide to the Galaxy* and I recommend you visit the one that does.

Anti-establishment emotions are good fodder for a spot of bracing vitriol; hence Abramovich's Chelsea are known as Chelski, and Man Utd supporters come in for a lot of stick due to the size and spread of their fan base. Home and away they will be asked in song, 'Do you come from Manchester?' To which the unspoken answer is often 'No, Bournemouth actually, but, honestly, I've supported them for years and my grandma once went to Lancashire to see her cousin'. However, this seems to matter less in the modern age.

There was a time when it was unthinkable to support anyone but your home team. Now, if you come from England's south coast, you might well support Man Utd, or Liverpool, or Arsenal, but perhaps not Workington FC or Bradford Park Avenue. Why is that?

Hence Arsenal fans at Old Trafford will begin singing (to 'She'll Be Coming Round the Mountain'), as the game draws to a close, 'We'll race you back to London, yes we will'. Fulham supporters, not normally known for their innovative singing at Craven Cottage, have informed the visiting Man Utd fans that they 'Live round the corner, you only live round the corner'. This appears to be a Fulham original and is one of the few that have been taken up by other fans when Man Utd visit. Mind you, I say visit – more like pop out for a newspaper and to see a game. They may not have travelled very far, which explains another chant: 'Home in five minutes, you'll all be home in five minutes'. Some of this, like that last sentence, is unfair. There remain legions of MUFC fans who are from the north-west region, and, anyway, Man Utd are now a global brand and they have loyal supporters from all over the place. Free country, isn't it, and you can support anyone you like can't you? Well, yes, except for Leicester City, of course, or 'And Leicester' as they are also known – because, at some point in the late 1960s, someone somewhere in an English football stadium heard the old favourite 'We hate Nottingham Forest, we hate Liverpool too, we hate Man United, but X we love you', and for reasons known only to them, changed it to 'We hate Nottingham Forest, we hate Liverpool too (and Leicester!)' and before you knew it, fans of every club in the league took it up.

There are limits to freedom and there appears to be universal agreement that we hate Leicester, even though, as discussed earlier, we don't really, and Gary Lineker definitely doesn't.

Where Manchester United Association Football Club does deserve stick is for its determination to rid Old Trafford of any atmosphere by insisting that, as soon as the referee blows the whistle to start ninety minutes of action-packed drama, everyone has to sit down during the game and read a book, meditate, swap stamps or some other such wholesome activity.

The club also, according to Roy Keane, serves prawn sandwiches in the executive box area instead of black pudding and tripe, as they clearly should, being, as they are, from Ecky Thump land. Now there's nothing wrong with the prawn sandwich, unless you're a prawn, or Jewish and religious, and they're not really even that posh, but Keane used it as an example of the yuppification of the game and it is now instantly recognisable shorthand.

I've read that Arsenal handed out an officially approved song-book in 2004. If true (I've never seen a copy), I hope it was in the spirit of documenting the Arsenal FC songs down through the years. If it was to tell fans what they should sing, then it was conceived by someone who, like manager Arsène Wenger, must live in hope, not expectation, of success.

Arsenal's stadium is one of those places where the club orders the stewards to tell everyone to sit down. A small but significant percentage of fans are either tourists from Asia, and so may think this is normal behaviour for a football fan, or are corporate-class fans who think they've paid £50 to watch the game and so everyone else should jolly well sit down and watch it. From a few sections of the stadium you hear the die-hard 'Gooners' trying their best to create something from this hushed 'atmosphere lite', while in the away end you hear 5,000 people having their own party. No wonder Arsenal's support is better away than at home.

Occasionally, if there are few away fans, say if Wigan visit, and the home crowd is a bit thin, during a break in play you can hear a strange crunching sound. This is not one of Jack Wilshere's late tackles, some of which are so late they take place after the game has ended: it's the sound of people eating crisps. I've been to The Emirates many times, and each time I become more convinced that Bono was writing about the Arsenal corporate affairs team in the U2 song which says that everyone except you is enjoying themselves, and goes on to mention the end of the world.

Corporate affairs types talk in a strange language, saying things like 'going forward' and believing that fans 'travel through the day's experience' when they mean 'in the future' and 'going to the game'. If it becomes about popping out during treatment for an injured player to get another overpriced Coke and a prawn baguette, before sitting down and not singing, then the core audience won't go any more. At that point the atmosphere will leave as well, and if the atmosphere goes, the TV will go, and if the TV goes, the money goes, and if the money goes, the top players go, etc.

Remember, if Ronaldo scores in an empty stadium – it may not be a goal.

At Everton's Goodison Park, fans sometimes generate a cracking atmosphere despite the repeated directions from the PA announcer that everyone should sit down. This is often directed at the away supporters, who are told that their ticket allocation for next season's game will be reduced if there continues to be 'persistent standing'. Persistent standing? Now there's a phrase conjured up by a Gollum-like Elf in Safety who wants to wrap his cold hands around the beating heart of football and squeeze the passion out of it.

Happily, at Old Trafford, many Man U fans stoically ignore the best efforts of the stewards to send everyone to sleep and they get stuck in. Sadly, this has resulted in some ridiculous standoffs and penalties for loyal football fans who were simply doing what people have been doing for 130 years now – enjoying the game after a long week at work. To their credit, and it gives me no pleasure to say this, Man Utd fans can, sometimes, create a decent atmosphere, with a wide repertoire of songs, even if 20 per cent of them do leave before the ninety minutes is up.

When that happens, the correct traditional response, by away fans, is to sing 'We can see you sneaking out', but hats off to Tottenham who, upon spotting Arsenal fans behaving in a similar manner, demanded to know 'Is there a fire drill? Is there a fire drill?' That was in 2012. By 2014 it had spread as far as the Midlands. In March 2014, Stoke were four–one up at Villa Park with ten minutes to go. So many Villa fans left in disgust that, by the ninetieth minute,

Stoke were singing the fire drill song to an empty stadium. It's now gone nationwide. There's a conflict of interest at moments like that, if it's you who wants to sneak out. On the one hand, you need to show your support for your club; at the same time, you need to register your disapproval, especially if some players look as if they're not trying hard enough. It must be horrendously embarrassing for top players to see everyone walking out on them.

Aston Villa picked up on Keane's sandwiches in April 2009. Thirty minutes into the first half, the away support spotted United fans leaving for refreshments and broke into the chant of 'Time for a sandwich, it must be time for a sandwich'. I'm indebted to midfielddynamo.com for that one and several others in this section.

* * *

Perhaps the most mined pit for humour is physical appearance. Hence Liverpool to Barcelona's snaggletoothed Ronaldinho at Anfield: 'Cilla wants her teeth back.' The Brazilian may not have known who Cilla Black is – I don't think she's very big in Rio Grande do Sul, where he grew up – but the Liverpool fans certainly enjoyed the moment.

The equally dentally challenged Luis Suárez, perhaps best known for sinking his gnashers into Chelsea's Branislav Ivanovic, is often informed, 'Your teeth are offside, your teeth are offside, Luis Suárez, your teeth are offside', but is reassured by The Kop that 'He's Luis Suárez, he bites who he wants.'

My mate Phil Hardacre wrote to me with a suggestion and said: 'Liverpool can have this one for free – "Luis Suárez: he looks like a donkey, but plays like Red Rum".' This is actually quite kind, as Red Rum was quality and, as we all know, when it comes to playing football, so is Suárez. However, I'm not sure it works. Liverpool fans were not about to call their beloved Uruguayan a donkey, and, anyway, he looks like a razor-toothed chipmunk, not a domesticated hoofed mammal of the horse family.

I've often thought that Andy Carroll's hair spends a good deal of time offside in any game it plays. If he's wearing his hair down, and it's a windy day, it's usually a foot beyond the last player and the linesman should flag. If his hair is up and he's got his back to goal, the bun is sometimes marginally offside. In fact, it's difficult to see how he can ever be level with the last defender, because even if he's level, his hair isn't, and somewhere in the FA rule book there must be something covering this. However, I've never questioned Carroll's gender, especially not to his face – he's huge. Others have, though; from the relative safety of the terraces, he is asked, 'Man or a woman? Are you a man or a woman?'

Wayne Rooney's hair weave attracts the chant, 'Who's the Scouser in the wig?', and Phil Thompson's nose came in for a lot of attention from away fans when it joined him on the Liverpool bench as part of the management team in the early 2000s. There were three songs in particular about his Roman features that stick in the memory: 'Get your nostrils off the pitch', 'Sit down Pinocchio', and 'He's got the whole world in his nose'. Thompson wasn't picky, he just ignored the abuse, as did, in the previous decade, the increasingly rotund Jan Mølby of Liverpool who, when warming up on the touchline, began to be greeted with 'Get your tits out for the lads'. He had massive potential for growth, fulfilled it, and then exceeded expectations with an even more dramatic weight gain when he lumbered into management.

Mark Viduka was always a big lad. The Celtic, Leeds and Newcastle striker could certainly fill his shirt, but, according to Spurs, his bottom half was quite big, too. 'They're by far the biggest shorts, the world has ever seen!' The former Everton and England midfielder Peter Reid once told me a story about Viduka that explains why, in between scoring fantastic goals, the Aussie often looked a little distracted. 'On my first day managing Leeds I was getting to know the players and Man U had been on the box the day before. So I asked Mark what he thought of the game and he said, "Dunno, I didn't watch, I don't really like football"!'

Nwankwo Kanu of Nigeria, Arsenal, West Brom and Portsmouth was a bit of an enigma. His age used to vary from game to game. Was he in his late twenties? Early thirties? Mid thirties? How come sometimes he ambled languidly around the pitch like a sixty-year-old, occasionally stopping for a mid-afternoon nap, but would suddenly burst into life as if he was in his prime, and score a top goal, before celebrating with an embarrassing Dad dance that went on for ages?

When he scored the winning goal in the 2008 FA Cup Final, manager Harry Redknapp joked that Kanu was forty-seven, but some people took him seriously. The other joke was that he enjoyed a decade at the top, aged between twenty-nine and thirty. It was a mystery not solved by the Portsmouth fans' chant: 'Oh Kanu, Kanu, He's older than me and you. He's a hundred and thirty-two. Oh Kanu, Kanu.' The official records state that Kanu was born on 1 August 1976, which is a birthday worth celebrating, as he was a terrific player and now does sterling charity work back home in Nigeria. Since retiring, he has never been seen moving any faster than a medium-paced walk.

Even a passing resemblance to anyone famous will spark a song. Thus Jimmy Floyd Hasselbaink was 'Just a fat Eddie Murphy' and Jonjo Shelvey, who, as well as playing for Liverpool and

Swansea, has also been accused of playing Voldemort in the Harry Potter films via the song: 'He's coming for you . . . He's coming for you, Harry Potter . . . He's coming for you.'

My December 2013 copy of *Scottish Review* informed me that the miserable Danish philosopher Søren Kierkegaard played in goal for Cowdenbeath FC, a team that hails from the region of West Fife. This really caught my attention, given that I'd always been fascinated by the fact that the equally miserable French existentialist writer Albert Camus actually did play in goal for Racing Universitaire Algerios. Sadly, reading down into the article, it transpired that the Kierkegaard–Cowdenbeath connection was only that the Blue Brazil's Allan Fleming is an absolute ringer for the great Dane. They have never been seen in the room as each other, but this may be because they are separated by 150 years. Even so, the likeness is so uncanny you could bring yourself to believe in reincarnation. It's a real shame Kierkegaard never played for Cowdenbeath: I like to think that the 'Father of Existentialism' would have been cheered up with a rousing chorus of 'Kierkegaard! Wooah oo oh. He knows the meaning of life. And now he plays in Fife.'

My favourite lookie-likey song is from Irish fans in Dublin who noticed that their fantastic defender Paul McGrath might look just a little bit like Nelson Mandela if you were in a dimly lit room, had had a few drinks and possessed a good imagination. The Irish team were due to return to Dublin from Italia 90, but on the same day, the late, great Nelson Mandela was in town to receive the Freedom of the City. According to former President of Ireland Mary McAleese, as quoted by the *Irish Examiner*, her daughter Sarah is responsible for one of the most warm, heartfelt and amusing chants ever. 'My three small children were anxious to see the Ireland team come home, but I persuaded them that the most historic thing they could do that day was to go and see Nelson Mandela [...] When he came out onto the Mansion House podium, Sarah started chanting: "Ooh, aah, Paul McGrath ..." The crowd immediately began to take up the call – but adding a rider to the original – and, within seconds, the whole area resounded with a chant of "Ooh aah, Paul McGrath's Da". When, as president years later, she met Mandela, she recounted the story and says he 'laughed heartily'.

Liverpool fans seem obsessed with the four-liner chants ending in someone's name. Some are funny, some surreal, some music-hall. For Peter Crouch, all nine foot four of him:

He's big,
He's red,
His feet stick out the bed,
Peter Crouch, Peter Crouch.

And for all four foot nine of Irishman Robbie Keane:

He's fast,
He's red,
He talks like Father Ted,
Robbie Keane, Robbie Keane.

In honour of manager Rafa Benitez' hirsute appearance:

It's neat,
It's weird,
Its Rafa's goatee beard,
Rafa's beard, Rafa's beard.

Arsenal had a good one when Frenchman Emmanuel Petit graced their midfield:

He's big,
He's quick,
His name's a porno flick,
Emmanuel, Emmanuel.

And West Ham came up with an obvious, but still funny, one for Adrian San Miguel:

He's big,
He's here,
His name's a Spanish beer,
San Miguel, San Miguel.

Pop songs offer a seemingly endless supply of tunes and words for the terraces, some more clever than others. My favourite is an obscure but brilliant reworking of a Beatles song by York City fans. The Minstermen had a striker from Nigeria named Onome Sympson Sodje. He went on to play for Partizani Tirana in the Albanian Superliga, but in the 2007/08 season Onome was City's top scorer, helping them to fourteenth place in the Football Conference. York fans serenaded their hero to the tune of 'Eleanor Rigby':

Onome Sodje.
He picks up the ball in the half where possession has been.
Has anyone seen?
Onome Sodje.

I can't quite work out why I like that one so much. 'Eleanor Rigby' was the B side to 'Yellow Submarine', which is sung by many a fan in many a stadium with many a change of words. 'Yellow Submarine' lends itself naturally to the terraces. But 'Eleanor Rigby'? It's a Lennon–McCartney piece of complex subtlety, and getting a football chant into it is to be applauded.

A close second, but a lot of people's favourite, is the Traoré song. It is a glorious celebration of a comedy own goal, scored by Liverpool's Djimi Traoré against Burnley. It's made all the funnier because the Liverpool fans themselves came up with it, borrowing from Michael Jackson's 'Blame It on the Boogie'.

Don't blame it on the Biscan
Don't blame it on the Finann
Don't blame it on the Hamann
Blame it on Traoré.
He just can't, he just can't, he just can't control his feet.

How 'His name is Rio – he watches from the stands' (about Rio Ferdinand's eight-month ban in 2003 for missing a drugs test) was voted 'funniest chant in a decade' by a website in early 2014 is beyond me. It's not even as good as the Newcastle United ode to their Senegalese right back, Habib Beye, using the tune from *Happy Days*:

Sunday, Monday, Habib Beye.
Tuesday, Wednesday, Habib Beye.
Thursday, Friday, Habib Beye.
Saturday, Habib Beye –
Rocking all week with you!

David Bowie's 'Rebel Rebel', not a bad song in itself, was improved at Old Trafford in honour of the Neville brothers, Phil and Gary:

Neville Neville, your future's immense,
Nevile Neville, you play in defence,
Neville Neville, like Jacko you're bad,
Neville Neville, is the name of your dad.

And it is. Gary and Phil Neville's dad is called Neville Neville. And a lot of people know that. Fewer know of Lenell John-Lewis, a lower leagues striker, who is frequently reminded that:

Your name is a shop
Lenell John-Lewis
Your name is a shop.

Many modern musicians are honoured if one of their songs receives the ultimate tribute of being transferred to the terraces as a chant, but I wonder what the late, great songwriter Ian Curtis would have made of his masterpieces making the journey. I can't divorce the blistering, hopeless, sadness of the Joy Division front man's 'Love Will Tear Us Apart' from his subsequent suicide. Nevertheless, the chorus is simple, melodic, and the words easy to change. Hence 'Giggs, Giggs will tear you apart, again' from Old Trafford for Ryan Giggs, which I think was the first use of the song, and 'Lovell tear you apart, again' at Aberdeen, when Steve Lovell played at Pittodrie. It's possible Leeds have missed a trick by not singing 'Leeds will tear you apart', but then again, it's probable that, even though it would work as a chant, it will never be adopted due to its association with that team from across the Pennines.

The demise of singer Michael Jackson inspired Marine FC fans to honour their local version of the global superstar with a rendition of 'Winter Wonderland'.

There's only Michael Jackson
One Michael Jackson
There used to be two
But now there's just you
Singing in a Jackson Neverland.

Old songs can always be revisited for new players. In 1982, Musical Youth had a hit with 'Pass the Dutchie' twenty-two years before Raheem Sterling was even born. But in the winger's first season at Liverpool, the song was back, this time from The Kop, with the lyrics:

Pass to Sterling on the left hand side
Pass to Sterling on the left hand side
He's gonna run
Give him the ball – let twist and turn
He's gonna run
Give him the ball – let twist and turn.

The Musical Youth version was actually an update of the original from 1981, by reggae group the Mighty Diamonds, and I mean the mighty, Mighty Diamonds, a class act from Jamaica. They had it as 'pass the kuchie', as in the marijuana, which even as late as 1982 was problematic for radio, so Musical Youth changed it to dutchie, which is slang for a cooking pot, but this didn't stop the rest of us knowing what they were on about.

If a hit is from a group connected with a team, it's always going to be taken up locally (hence Man City's 'Wonderwall'). The Kaiser Chiefs have openly admitted not only being from Leeds, but also to supporting Leeds United, so 'I Predict a Riot' always gets a good sing-along on the PA at Elland Road. At away games, on very rare occasions, Leeds fans have a version of another Kaiser Chiefs hit, 'Oh My God', singing 'we've never been this good away from home'. The band, by the way, took their name from the former club of Leeds player Lucas Radebe, who was from Soweto in South Africa.

Even Adam and the Ants get a terrace mention, proving that Adam was right all along – ridicule is nothing to be scared of. The difference between this song and the others is that he's named-checked, not quoted. Man City, Sunderland and Sheffield Wednesday can argue about who came up with this first, with Niall Quinn or David Hirst as the subject (and they do).

Niall Quinn's disco pants are the best;
They go up from his arse to his chest.
They are better than Adam and the Ants,
Niall Quinn's . . . disco pants.

Or, if you prefer, insert David Hirst's name.

Timing is everything. One of Man City's best chants was timed to the first home game after City keeper Joe Hart, who must have been down to his last million, decided to make a comical 'Wash 'n Go' advert to promote an anti-dandruff product. It took just minutes before, to the 'Yaya Touré' chant, nicked from 2Unlimited's *No Limits*, the fans came up with 'No, no, no, no. No, no, no, no. No, no, no, no, no, no Dandruff!', followed up by, to the tune of 'Chirpy Chirpy Cheep Cheep': 'Where's your dandruff gone? Where's your dandruff gone?'

The Manchester City wags were also responsible for chanting 'You're not incredible' at Porto's Givanildo Vieira de Souza 'Hulk', and the same lot, when asked by Millwall 'Does the Social know you're here?', responded with 'Do you know your father's name?' Arsenal's contribution when playing Porto was to chant at Hulk, 'Green in a minute – you're going green in a minute'.

City fans seem to specialise in pop songs. Georgi Kinkladze was a midfield favourite at the same time as Man City fans Oasis were at their height. The song for the Georgian was taken from the single 'Wonderwall' – 'And all the runs that Georgi makes are winding. And all the girls in Manchester are blinding'. City also took Pink Floyd's *The Wall*, and the Manchester slang for the police, and came up with:

We don't need no police protection.
We don't need no ground control.
Hey Dibble!
Leave those kids alone.

You can't be sure about these things, but it's thought that Dibble comes from the Top Cat cartoon featuring the hapless Officer Dibble character.

Crystal Palace fans have a more aggressive version of the Floyd song – 'All in all – you're just a bunch of pricks in Millwall'. Abusive? Obscene? Clever? Funny? That's mostly down to individual preference. I don't have strong feelings about it either way. Terrace culture, or to stretch the point a bit, working-class male humour, is often rougher than other sections of society, because working-class life is rougher. The humour is sharp and reflects where it comes from. All the same, Hillsborough/Munich songs cross the invisible lines most of have in our heads, so do the 'funny' chants about Jimmy Savile, Fred West, the Yorkshire Ripper and the Moors Murderers. Bellowing obscenities about the torture and murder of children in recent times just isn't funny, nor is 'taking ownership' of someone local like Savile (as Leeds fans have done), to turn the chants directed at them from other supporters back around. It doesn't turn them around; it just makes those who began them feel legitimised.

Rightly or wrongly, there is clearly a statute of limitations about the most grotesque behaviour by humans, and when you can or can't start joking about it. Raping and pillaging by Vikings has been staple comedy fare, probably for centuries; the Arabs will make flippant remarks about the Mongol hordes totally destroying Baghdad and killing hundreds of thousands of people in the process; and Vlad the Impaler – well, he's meat and drink to many a comic. However, with Savile and West *et al*, we are dealing with our time, our generation and our people. So, if you're looking for the Fred West and Saddleworth Moor jokes and chants, look elsewhere. Or rather, don't: you'll only encourage them.

Compared to that, the following is tame, but much more of a laugh. Most of us know which is more important, given a choice between having a laugh and proving you're the nastiest bastard around. Humour can be cruel. It also doesn't need to let facts get in the way, even if the subject is a mental disability. The most famous example of this is the Andy Goram chant. When the then Rangers and Scotland goalkeeper was helpful enough to tell people about how he coped with a mild form of schizophrenia, football fans didn't bother to read up on what schizophrenia actually is. What it is not is a split personality, but no matter – 'Two Andy Gorams, there's only two Andy Gorams' is a legendary terrace chant and regularly voted among the funniest.

Less well known, but in the same vein, was the Man Utd song in honour of their keeper Tim Howard, who suffered from a very mild version of Tourette's syndrome, which, when severe, brings severe tics and can involve involuntary swearing. The Stretford End responded with:

Timmy Howard
Fuck off!
He plays in our net
Fuck off!
Timmy Howard
Fuck off!
He's got Tourette's.

This may not display an informed appreciation of what Mr Tourette first diagnosed, nor may it be helpful in understanding what the disease can entail, but, like many a borderline song, it does not appear to be born of malice.

We occasionally can be persuaded to drop our utter contempt for the woolly backs/Cockney monkeys/northern savages/sheep shaggers/Wurzels/Jocks/inbreeds, etc., at the other end of the stadium and actually recognise the humour in their chants. Not often, but it does happen. If your team has gone two–nil up with twenty minutes to go, and looks as if it may be on the way to winning its first away game in twelve attempts, it is important to sing 'We're winning away, we're winning away – how shit must you be? We're winning away'. You need to get this in quickly, though, as the home side will probably bang in two goals to secure the draw.

However, if you were playing Manchester United between 1986 and 2013, you'd lose three–two, as they would probably have scored in 'Fergie Time'. This was a rip in the space–time continuum caused by a temporal effect on Alex Ferguson's chewing gum that would emit a strange force which caused the referee's stop watches at Old Trafford to. Stop. Mysteriously. Stop. Like that. Then, they would start again as soon as Man Utd had scored, time would speed up and the game would end. It was very odd.

However, if it wasn't Man Utd you were playing, then your chant of 'We're winning away' would be met by the home fans, especially in the lower leagues, with 'We lose every week, we lose every week, you're nothing special, we lose every week'.

Self-deprecatory humour was taken to extremes by Brighton fans when the club signed all five foot three of Dean Cox; they welcomed him with the chant of 'We've got tiny Cox – I said we've got tiny Cox'. His little ditty has followed Mr Cox to each of his clubs. That reminds me, when Wigan brought on a diminutive sub at White Hart Lane, the Spurs fans sang 'Why's the mascot on the pitch?' He was then booked for a foul which the Spurs fans felt deserved a red card, resulting in a change of words – 'Get the mascot off the pitch'.

It is possible to be self-deprecatory and celebratory at the same time. Wigan responded to Liverpool's boast about the European Cup, 'We've won it five times', with 'We've won it two times; we've won it two times. The Auto Windscreens trophy, we've won it two times'.

When Mohamed Al-Fayed was the owner of Fulham FC and was having trouble applying for a passport, the fans came up with

'Al-Fayed – whooah oh oh. Al-Fayed – wooah oh oh. He wants to be a Brit, and QPR are shit'.

Then there are evergreens, a chant for all seasons. Our ever-expanding waistlines ensure that 'Who ate all the pies, who ate all the pies? You fat bastard, you fat bastard, you ate all the pies' will continue to resound year in, year out, as will 'You've never seen a salad'. Any ne'er-do-well player convicted, or even accused, of criminal activity can still be expected to be told 'You're supposed to be in jail'.

However, some of the best one-liners are one-offs, sung on the day, in the moment, leaving behind only a memory and a satisfying childish smirk. For example: Peterborough v. Leeds in League One. In the open area right in front of the London Road stadium, fans were treated to the sight of two mobile chlamydia testing vans, with signs inviting them to go in for a consultation. You can imagine the reaction – 'Hang on, lads, just popping in for a quick chlamydia test'. Or not. The Peterborough staff were handing out flyers, and the toilets were festooned with posters and leaflets extolling everyone to get a grip on themselves in that department.

At the time, the Leeds manager was Gary McAllister. The away fans, after spending the first ten minutes abusing the Peterborough manager, Darren Ferguson, son of that other manager, came up with an absolute belter, with which the entire away end joined in. 'We've got McAllister, You've got chlamydia'.

What I expect was another one-off was sung by Spurs fans at a midweek away game in the UEFA Cup. It was Valentine's Day, so everyone should have known the answer to the question: 'Where should the fans be on this romantic night?'

The answer was either: A – At home with their WAGs or, increasingly these days, HABs, or B – At the game. The answer came through in the first half, loud and clear, and in the knowledge that it could be heard via the TV speakers in North London – 'We love Tottenham, we love Tottenham, we love Tottenham more than you!' The following night there were probably several conversations in North London along the lines of 'Did you sing that?' – 'Of course not, darling.'

The Man Utd protest at the Glazers' takeover of the club led to thousands of fans abandoning the red and white for a season and wearing the old gold and green of Newton Heath, as the club was known when it first formed in 1878. That season, when Norwich City came calling, the Canaries' fans adopted the Beach Boys hit 'Sloop John B' and broke out into a somewhat sublime, slightly surreal song after noticing the similarity with their own colours:

We've come for our scarves,
We've come for our scarves,
We're Norwich City,
We've come for our scarves.

At Hull, fans were proud, and, I am assured, not in the least bit surprised, when one Friday afternoon in 2013 their hometown was named UK City of Culture for 2017. The home of abolitionist William Wilberforce, the annual Freedom Festival, Philip Larkin, Throbbing Gristle, The Housemartins, Maureen Lipman, Mick Ronson and Uncle Tom Courtenay and all won't receive any government funding for this, but locals hope the honour will continue the city's recent regeneration after decades in the doldrums. On the Saturday following the Friday, Crystal Palace came to visit, and Hull fans welcomed the poor benighted Cockneys with 'Here for the culture, you're only here for the culture'.

Speaking of which, Bradford City fans don't often get the opportunity to see their team play Ajax of Amsterdam, and so, naturally, when they did, they took the one-off opportunity to sing 'Did you bring us, did you bring us, did you bring us any drugs?'

In the 1970s the wonderfully talented Stanley Bowles of QPR was playing an away game at Anfield. Stanley had two other first names that were attached to just about every sentence written about him, 'Mercurial', and 'Maverick', and that was about him both on and off the pitch. A manager once said of him, 'If Stan could pass a betting shop like he can pass a football, he'd be all right.' On the day of the Liverpool game, the papers were full of stories that Anne, the long-suffering wife of Mercurial Maverick Stanley Bowles, had left him. He was in midfield, but couldn't miss the chant that came out of The Kop, given that perhaps ten thousand people were singing it:

> *Where's yer wife gone*
> *Where's yer wife gone*
> *Where's yer wife gone – Stanley Bowles?*

Stanley turned to The Kop, thought about the question for a couple of seconds, and then, with perfect comic timing, gave an exaggerated shrug.

On another occasion a cat ran onto the pitch at Anfield and The Kop changed the 'Attack Attack' chant into 'A cat. A cat. A cat. A cat. A cat!' It has happened at other grounds, but I doubt you get more than one chance at that chant in a lifetime.

Wolves had a one-off opportunity and took it when there was a total ban on Cardiff fans coming to Molineux. They directed an old favourite towards a completely empty away end: 'You're not singing any more. You're not singing any more.' Like any decent striker, you need to take your chances when they come.

If any fan is romantic enough to propose on the pitch, or even get married in the centre circle at half time, it is customary to sing 'You don't know what you're doing. You don't know what you're doing.' I've only seen this once, but it does happen.

If, as West Brom fans did, when inside Orient's Brisbane Road stadium, you spot some people in the windows of nearby flats, you can break into a chant of 'We can see you, we can see you, we can see you washing up'.

News events can spark one-off chants. When Northern Rock building society, sponsor of Newcastle United, went bust, Derby Country fans greeted Newcastle supporters with: 'Banked with the Woolwich. You should have banked with the Woolwich.' More recently, when the West Country was inundated and parts of it cut off, away fans visiting local clubs showed their concern by singing 'Flooded in the morning. You're getting flooded in the morning.'

The news can also teach us about the cultures of other people. Before the statue of Saddam Hussein came down in Baghdad in 2003, who knew the Arabs took their shoes off in order to show their contempt for something by beating it with the soles of the footwear? And who would have thought that, a decade later, Leeds fans would take to removing their shoes, waving them in the air, and singing 'Shoes off – if you hate Man U'.

Another aspect of international culture is, of course, food. Turkish cuisine, for instance, has long held football fans' attention in the shape of the kebab, preferably served with chilli sauce and near a taxi rank. Chelsea fans displayed their knowledge of this Turkish delight when Galatasaray visited, by chanting at the away fans: 'You're Shish! And you know you are.'

Apologies for that brief interruption, now we return to the news. In 1999, Graham Rix, the former Arsenal and England midfielder, was found guilty of having sex with an under-age girl. She was fifteen; he testified that he thought she was sixteen. Either way, he served six months of a twelve-month sentence. After doing his time he came out, got back into football and ended up managing Heart of Midlothian in Edinburgh. This spurred the rival Hibernian fans to come out with a chant to the tune of the Manic Street Preachers' song 'If You Tolerate This Your Children Will Be Next', only substituting the word 'Rix' for 'This'.

The unlikely revelation that Osama bin Laden was an Arsenal fan on his brief visit to London as a teenager, resulted in a Gunners chant of:

Osama, woooah.
Osama, woooah.
He follows Arsenal.
He's hiding in Kabul.

The back pages of the tabloids are always useful fodder for a topical chant, as is the tune to 'Lord of the Dance'. Chelsea fans paid tribute to their captain, John Terry, after noticing his friendship with the wife of former teammate Wayne Bridge: 'Chelsea, Chelsea, Wherever you may be, Keep your wife from John Terry.'

'Que Sera Sera' is good for a song, especially for Aston Villa players who might go to lap-dancing clubs after beating Ajax in 2008, and who also have one syllable in their first name and two in the second:

John Carew, Carew.

He likes a lap dance or two.
He might even pay for you.
John Carew, Carew.

The physical exertions of Sven-Göran Eriksson have been noticed by the back pages, the front pages and by every football fan in the country. At one point he was in charge at Man City, and male City fans were so impressed by the Swedish lothario's efforts, and managerial abilities, that they changed the 'Lord of the Dance' to:

Sven, Sven, wherever you may be.
You are the pride of Man City.
You can shag my wife, on our settee.
If we get to Wembley.

It would take a team of highly paid psychoanalysts to unravel that one, but it seems to be based on the dubious premise, on behalf of those singing, that they love their club, they love their wives, and greater love hath no man than he lay down his wife for his club. The views of said wives may not have been taken into account during the singing of this song and I doubt they were present on the terraces, although you can't rule it out.

Some Swindon Town supporters had a similar song and a similar view of love and devotion. When Paolo Di Canio was their manager, he used to demonstrate his passion for the game by sliding to his knees on the rare occasions when his team scored a goal. Even if he was wearing a £1,000 suit from Ermenegildo Zegna, and it was muddy, and raining, he would scoot out of the technical area, sink to his knees, and glide along the touchline. Naturally, therefore, to the tune of the 1967 hit 'Can't Take My Eyes Off You' by Frankie Valli, the Swindon fans would sing:

Paolo Di Canio, you are the love of my life
Paolo Di Canio, I'd let you shag my wife
Paolo Di Canio
'Cos I want dirty knees too.

I prefer this one to the Man City version, as it is saves us the vision of Sven by candlelight on a fan's settee in the Manchester suburb of Chorlton-cum-Hardy. It also has a better punch line. However, I am again doubtful that Mrs Football Fan was consulted. Mind you, it's possible that one or two might have said yes, if asked. Neither Di Canio nor Eriksson look the like the back end of a bus, although one does have the unfortunate tendency to raise his right arm in an ugly manner.

Ahh, there were once more gentle times, times when manager Brian Clough could put a sign up in the Nottingham Forest penalty area before a match saying 'No swearing please – Brian'. It was a one-off day, and for the day, for once, it wasn't just the teams who played ball. The Trent End, instead of calling into question the referee's parentage, sang: 'You're a naughty, you're a naughty, you're a naughty referee . . .', and, with reference to the reasons why a player might have missed an open goal: 'A shot – he's missed – he must be rather drunk . . .' Bless. That was a time of wine and roses for Cloughie.

These days modern Britain gets some of its bacchanalian delights from Colombia. I need to say here that Sheffield United, QPR and Leeds goalkeeper Paddy Kenny does not indulge in Colombia's biggest export. However, in May 2009, he had imbibed a cough medicine containing a tiny amount of ephedrine, which, alas, falls foul of the FA's rules on performance-enhancing drugs. Poor Paddy was banned from playing for nine months. He's also had to put up with a song paying tribute to his love of a good time, which has followed him around ever since: 'Paddy Kenny – is having a party. Bring some vodka. And your charlie.'

Fans of a certain vintage will remember the old hooligan chant warning away fans that 'You're going home in a fucking ambulance'. During the 1989 limited ambulance strike, the army took over and the chant was changed to 'You're going home in an army ambulance'. Every referee in the country is reminded at least once during a game that 'You're not fit to referee', but Arsenal fans take credit for singing it when it was indisputable, as referee Mark Clattenburg was being treated on the pitch for an injury.

The earliest one-off I know of goes back to 1967, when Leeds keeper Gary Sprake threw the ball into his own net, in front of the Kop. The crooner Des O'Connor had recorded a top ten hit single earlier that year and within seconds of Sprake's mistake, the Kop was serenading him with 'Careless Hands', originally a Tin Pan Alley hit written in 1948 by Carl Sigman and Bob Hilliard, and yet another song that crossed the Atlantic west to east and ended up on the terraces, albeit briefly. A few years after Gary Sprake's mishap there was another one-off song, equally cruel, arguably funnier.

Asa Hartford, the West Brom and Scotland midfielder, was on the verge of signing for Leeds United when the medical tests, normally a formality, suggested he had a hole in his heart. It was a deal breaker, but not for Man City, who snapped him up and with whom he had a successful career. The following season, when City came to Elland Road, the Gelderd End sang 'There's a hole in your heart, dear Asa, dear Asa, there's a hole in your heart, dear

Asa, a hole'. Most clubs followed suit and the chant went with him around the grounds for a year. That was deliberate, certainly more deliberate than TV commentator David Coleman's howler during the 1978 World Cup in Argentina when, after several mentions of Hartford's condition, he managed to describe him as a 'whole-hearted player' before getting in an apology snappier than a Graeme Souness tackle.

Many songs last only as long as a player's career. For more than a decade, fans have enjoyed watching Bobby Zamora play for Bristol Rovers, Spurs, West Ham, Fulham and QPR, and even twice for England. Bobby can strike the ball really hard, he can really hit it, but not always in the direction he intends, which explains the song that has followed him around from stadium to stadium, sung to 'That's Amore': 'When you're sat in Row Z, And the ball hits your head, That's Zamora!'

This is sung in the perfect knowledge, of every one of us who goes to football matches, that we would have scored, so why on earth did Bobby, or whoever, miss that sitter? With our depth of understanding of the game, and our visionary vision, we are perfectly qualified to tell the players what they should and shouldn't be doing. I'm quite serious about this. If you've paid to get in, you are perfectly entitled to have an opinion. Even if your own footballing career only got as far as the school second eleven before that unfortunate injury at the age of sixteen, you know that you know more about the game than many of the players, as they are younger than you are, and if wasn't for that injury . . .

This explains why at games we shout at them 'Pass it wide!' or 'Skin him!' and 'Shoot!' All this is understandable and acceptable football behaviour. After all, it's mostly just an expression of the moment, what we want to happen, and of course, in reality, we don't really think we know more than the player. The exception to that was Paul Scholes in an England shirt – then it was acceptable to bellow at him, if he went within a yard of an opposing player – 'Don't tackle him!' – as it always ended badly.

However, there is an exception to our understanding of our own limitations, and he's been following me around football stadiums for decades. You may have seen him yourself at games, and in his own seat he is the world's leading authority on football tactics. He's usually sitting either two rows in front or behind you or me. He wears a variety of disguises. Sometimes he looks as if he's in his fifties, sometimes in his thirties, sometimes he has dark hair, sometimes fair hair, often no hair. I'm told he's from a large family and his twin brothers show up at games in Italy, Germany, Spain and Paraguay, in fact everywhere where football is played.

About ten minutes into the game he says, in a loud voice: 'They need to move von Dazzler further into midfield; he's not getting the ball.' As the minutes pass, he gets louder and louder. Eventually he's shouting, so that people up to twenty rows away can hear: 'Get it on the deck ya bastards, this lot can't run, we can beat them if we pass and move but they're too good in the air. Dazzler! Use the wings!'

A quick glance is enough to establish that this is not Joseph Morewhineo hamming it up on the terraces, and is in fact the bloke who follows you around everywhere. Sadly it's not often that the players or manager can hear him, so his pearls of wisdom fall on the stony ground of our irritation. His intermittent commentary continues for most of the game, and only stops when the striker – who he's been saying should never have been signed, and who now ought to be substituted – smashes a thirty-yard screamer into the net with ten minutes to go.

"Dirty Northern Bastards!"

One of his twin brothers is usually two-thirds of the way down the terracing behind the goal, wearing a replica shirt and a red face. If the fans aren't singing loudly enough, or just not to his liking, he gets ever redder in the face until his patience with us is exhausted. He turns round to face the terracing and shouts, 'Sing, ya bastards!' Standing near him is a bit like being on the front row at a stand-up comedy routine; you hope he doesn't zero in on you as being particularly to blame for not singing loudly enough to inspire the players to win. If we don't obey his command, the red becomes a worrying shade of purple and he begins bellowing, 'Sing! Fucking sing, ya bastards, won't you?!' before giving up, sitting down and ruminating about people's lack of passion. He's usually drunk. Anyway, he's all right really, because he supports the same team as you and me. He's free to feel indignant and we're free to ignore him. Even the twin brother a few seats along, impersonating the assistant manager, is OK, as he joins in the singing.

The more people who sing, and the louder the song, the greater the chance that those at whom it is directed will hear. This is very important. There's not much point in telling the inbred troglodytes with criminal tendencies 100 yards away behind the other goal that you find them morally objectionable, if they can't hear you. It would be like the adage in support of advertising: selling a product without advertising it is like winking at a beautiful woman in a dark room. You know you're doing it, but no one else does.

Ditto the players. What's the point of reminding them of the penalty they missed in the World Cup three years ago if they don't hear it, and thus are not psychologically damaged for ninety minutes and so do not score against your club? On a more positive note, the players also need to hear the songs of love and devotion, thus inspiring them to win and send you home happy. They really should make the best of it while they can, because very few players are still honoured from the terraces once their careers are over. There will come a day when Jermaine Easter, of Wycombe Wanderers, Millwall and other clubs, will no longer hear 'You're not as good as Christmas'; and even now, Blackburn Rovers fans can no longer sing to Roque Santa Cruz that 'Santa Cruz is coming to town'.

If you move down a couple of leagues into the semi-professional game, a player's day job can usually supply inspiration. Windsor and Eton FC fans marked Dave Tilbury's two-hundredth appearance with:

We've got Dave Tilbury,
He'll paint your house for free,
He quotes and estimates,
He paints and decorates.

Most players love it when a song is sung in their honour. In the top flight, the pay gap between them and us is enormous, but once they take to the pitch the physical distance between us is only a few yards, and a chant can be a great leveller.

Being reminded by thousands of people that your form is poor, week in, week out, via 'What a waste of money', has to get inside a striker's head at some point. Conversely, having stood on the terraces themselves as boys and sung the songs of praise, it must be a huge boost for your confidence and ego to hear your name chanted in a positive manner – more so, perhaps, if it's an original just for you. Lots of players get 'One Johnny Footballer'; some lucky ones get more.

Huddersfield Town fans used the staple fare of 'Sloop John B' as their tune for striker Lee Novak, but came up with a lyric to match anything written by Brian Wilson of The Beach Boys:

We've got Novak,
We've got Nova-a-ak,
Our carpets are filthy,
We've got Novak.

Ex-Chelsea player Nigel Spackman says the pace, concentration and noise involved in playing football means that not all songs for players are heard, but some are. 'You normally hear them in a stop in play, or your team mates, even during a game, might say, "Did you hear that one?" And they laugh. Having your name chanted by your own fans is a real positive, it's recognition that they appreciate you, that they relate to you and, as a footballer, it can make you stronger. It's recognition of what you give to them and their team and when their team is our team, we're playing for them.'

Conversely the negative chant can also have an effect, but not always the one the fans intend. Spackman tells a story of when he transferred to Liverpool from Chelsea: 'The Chelsea fans at Anfield were booing me and at half time [manager] Kenny Dalgleish said to me, "You know why they're booing you?" and I said, "'Cos I left Chelsea", and he said, "No. They're booing you because they know you're a top player." Some players are weakened by abuse but some are inspired, it depends on personality. More and more in the modern game you need to be mentally strong. It's about self belief, inner confidence.'

Barnsley fans had an abundance of that during the year in which they were happy in the Premier League, despite shipping eighty-two goals. They are often credited with coming up with 'It's just like watching Brazil' either during that season or the one before. At many clubs, this morphed into a greeting for the police when they walked in a line behind the goal – 'It's just like watching *The Bill*', but fair play to QPR for taking it another step in honour of one of their granite-like defenders: 'Clint Hill! – We just like watching Clint Hill! We just like watching Clint Hill! We just like watching Clint Hill!'

Aberdeen midfielder Peter Pawlett was honoured with a version of the Human League hit 'Don't You Want Me, Baby?' The chant, 'Peter Pawlett, baby!' is simplicity itself; same tune, six syllables for six syllables, but there's something joyful about it.

If you watch the footage of the post-match celebrations from the 2014 Scottish League Cup final, won by Aberdeen, you see the sheer delight on the faces of the Aberdeen players as 40,000 Dons supporters erupt into an impressively melodic rendition. Pawlett couldn't play in Aberdeen's first Cup Final for fourteen years due to injury, but he was on the pitch for the party. (Everton also picked up the Human League song for their injured Costa Rican defender Bryan Oviedo, with 'Oviedo, baby!') Aberdeen fans followed up their success with a social media campaign, which resulted in the original song going into the top ten new entries on the iTunes chart.

Many Queen songs have a certain anthemic quality. By adding their Japanese player's name to 'Radio Gaga', Man Utd came up with: 'All we need is Shinji Kagawa, Shinji Kagawa.'

Chelsea's César Azpilicueta presented something of a problem, given that he has a name not everyone can pronounce and which goes on forever. Someone at the Bridge came up with chant worthy of an honourable mention, but it never really took off, perhaps due to the word Azpilicueta being included in it.

We'll just call you Dave,
We'll just call you Dave,
Azpilicueta
We'll just call you Dave.

The Chelsea fans should take inspiration from Wrexham supporters, who have been known to bring a smile to faces with mention,
and correct pronunciation, of the longest one-word club name in
the UK and probably the world.

'Are you Llanfairpwllgwyngyllgogerychwyrndrobwllllantysiliogogogoch in disguise?'

Most of us, if we find the need, refer to Clwb Pel Droed
Llanfairpwllgwyngyllgogerychwyrndrobwllllantysiliogogogoch
simply as Llanfairpwll FC, which is hard enough to pronounce,
but not as hard as Llanfairpwllgwyngyllgogerychwyrndrobwllllantysiliogogogoch.

Llanfairpwllgwyngyllgogerychwyrndrobwllllantysiliogogogoch FC's ground is near Bangor and Llanfairpwllgwyngyllgogerychwyrndrobwllllantysiliogogogoch FC play in the
Welsh Alliance League. You may have got the pronunciation of
Llanfairpwllgwyngyllgogerychwyrndrobwllllantysiliogogogoch,
by now, but just in case, it's Llanfairpwllgwyngyllgogerychwyrndrobwllllantysiliogogogoch. (Usual spelling.)

Unlike Llanfairpwllgwyngyllgogerychwyrndrobwllllantysiliogogogoch, all good things come to an end, including Kerry
Mayo's professional career at the age of thirty-two due to a groin
injury in 2009. So, Brighton fans can no longer remind him that,
due to him marrying a woman called Kerry, there are only 'Two
Kerry Mayos'. Happily Kerry (the male one) was fit enough to go
into non-league football a year later. He signed for Newhaven and

told the local media: 'I'll still be putting myself about as much as my groin will allow'.

Due to his unfortunate transfer, we have already lost the biblical chant about Victor Moses when he was at Crystal Palace:

Oh Moses whooh oh oh
Oh Moses whooah oh oh
He comes from Norbury
He parted the Red Sea.

Moses, the son of Christian ministers, moved on to play for the Red side in Liverpool and unsuccessfully set about putting the ferry across the Mersey out of business.

Arsenal's Eduardo Alves da Silva was almost put out of business via a horror tackle by Birmingham City's Martin Taylor in 2008. Thankfully he made a full recovery and was able to go on to hear fans of rival clubs suggesting he was now playing in a manner akin to Paul McCartney's former wife, who has managed to forge a successful modelling career despite having a prosthetic leg:

Eduardo oh oh woah oh.
Eduardo oh oh woah oh
He used to have silky skills
Now he walks like Heather Mills.

Cruel. And what to make of the clever, cruel, and only partially based on fact, chant about the former Man Utd midfielder Park Ji-Sung ,who is from South Korea. Man U fans liked him so much they came up with a triple whammy. Praise for Park via the song, a joke at the expense of the entire South Korean population, and a dig at the Scousers:

> *Park, Park wherever you may be*
> *You eat dogs in your country*
> *But it could be worse*
> *You could be Scouse*
> *Eating rats in your council house.*

Another delicacy served up by the Stretford End was:

> *He shoots*
> *He scores*
> *He eats Labradors*
> *Park Ji-Sung, Park Ji-Sung.*

And not just Labradors apparently:

> *Ten Alsatians walking down the street,*
> *Ten Alsatians walking down the street,*
> *And if Park-Ji Sung should fancy one to eat*
> *There'll be nine Alsatians walking down the street.*

You may not be able to stomach that, in which case you'd be in the good company of South Korean men and women, the vast majority of whom also cannot abide dog meat. Some campaign against the practice.

But yes, some do go in for Fido and chips. It's estimated that up to 30 per cent of South Koreans have tried it and about 8 per cent eat Rover on a regular basis. And what's wrong with that,

I hear hardly anyone say. Certainly not the South Korean Man Utd fan who once led the singing of the first two canine songs above, while in the Bishop Blaize pub near Old Trafford.

Apart from the taste, there's not much difference between eating a pig and eating a dog (or so I'm told). I admit pigs won't fetch sticks, or bark at burglars, which is partly why, in the West, we eat them and not man's best friend, but in the Korean Peninsula, dogs are not man's best friend and there is no reason why they should feel emotionally about them in the way that we do. Perhaps they throw sticks for pigs to fetch? Oh, and while on the subject, I should mention dog stew, or 'Boshintang' as it is known in downtown Seoul, which is rumoured to be popular with gentlemen of a certain age who think it's the DBs and will be of assistance to them.

So, the three songs above are based on stereotypes, not fully backed up by evidence. The first is true, dogs are eaten in Korea, but the second is not so accurate. Park Ji-Sung does not eat Labradors. How he feels about Corgi with fava beans and a nice chianti is unknown.

Scotland fans also display a healthy culinary interest. On arrival in Paris, the skirt wearers will regale their beret-wearing old allies with 'We're the famous Tartan Army and we're here to save the snail' and will then gather beneath the Eiffel Tower to sing 'Big fucking pylon, it's just a big fucking pylon'. They have a point, but then again, so did Gustav Eiffel. When in Rome, instead of doing what the Romans do, they threaten to 'Deep fry your pizza, we're gonna deep fry your pizza', before heading north to Norway and reverting to their deep concern for the animal kingdom with the song 'Sing when you're whaling, you only sing when you're whaling'. (Speaking of Wales, if playing the Welsh, the Scots will sing 'We hate, we hate England, we hate England more than you!')

Celtic fans on an away day to the wealthy delights of Monaco came up with an excellent take on the 'In your slums' song:

In your Monaco slums,
You look through the dustbins for something to eat . . .
You find a dead lobster and think it's a treat
In your Monaco slums.

Some of those comedians may have been among the Scotland fans in Tallinn, who used the traditional version of a well-known football song but in highly unusual circumstances. The Estonian team had refused to take to the pitch due to some dispute or other, and the Scots came up with 'One team in Tallinn, there's only one team in Tallinn'.

Ah, the Tartan Army. What jokers. I remember going to see Scotland play Wales in Wrexham one day in the late 1970s when there must have been nothing on telly. I was with three Scottish friends exiled in the Midlands and keen to reassure me that as long as I kept quiet, didn't sing Jerusalem or burn the Saltire, I would be fine. We boarded a train in Wolverhampton, along with 700 other Scots in exile, 5,000 cans of McEwan's lager, and several sets of bagpipes.

About 100 yards out of Wolverhampton the train erupted with the chant 'If you hate the fuckin English, hate the fuckin English, hate the fuckin English clap yer hands!' They returned to the theme every few minutes. All the way to Wrexham. Oh how my friends laughed. Oh how my hands hurt from clapping. On the plus side I did learn about the Highland clearances, the Battle of Bannockburn and the words to that fine song 'Flower of Scotland'.

On arrival we went to the pub, then another pub, and then

another one. After that we went to the pub. And then it stopped being funny. One of my friends had thought it would be a wizard wheeze if he lent me his silk Rangers scarf to wear to the game to make up for the fact that I didn't have a tartan scarf. I did question the validity of said club totem, but was assured that it would be fine. It wasn't.

I'd not worn it on the train, but in pub four, with things getting very messy, the whole place erupting in singing, and beer being tossed around, I felt I should enter into the spirit of things, threw discretion to the winds, and took out the scarf.

Within five minutes a very large, overweight man in his forties detached himself from a group of similar looking friends, came over to me at the bar and said, 'Heei Hoowa heeo whoah fuckin hee hoowa whoo fuckin chib ye'. No, he really did say that, or at least to my ears that's what he said and I'm usually pretty good with accents. I resisted the temptation to start singing 'Speak fucking English, why don't you speak fucking English?' and instead, with a trembling bottom lip, simply replied, 'Sorry?' He repeated word for word what he'd said, and again the only bit I got was 'fuckin' and 'fuckin chib ye'.

I turned to my companions for subtitles and noticed they'd turned pale. What my new friend had said was 'If you don't take that fucking scarf from round your neck I'm going to fucking chib you' – that's 'chib you' as in 'razor you'.

The scarf came off, we left the pub, and my friends accepted that perhaps the joke wasn't as funny as it had seemed earlier, given that all of us may have been seconds from being stabbed. I was then given another crash course in Scottish history, the depths of the differences between Celtic and Rangers, and the assurance that, without doubt, the gentleman who'd taken the trouble to let me see the error of my ways was a Celtic fan, was probably a Catholic, and it was a reasonable assumption that he did indeed have a razor.

Not that I hold any grudges. Which reminds me: any particularly useless goalkeeper who lets in more than one goal, and has made an error, may be regaled with 'Scotland's Scotland's number one, Scotland's number one!' Sadly this is going out of fashion and being replaced with 'Two–nil – it's your keeper's fault'. This may be because the under-thirties have not been sufficiently educated in just how spectacularly poor Scotland's goalkeepers were in the 1980s. Naturally, fans of Scottish clubs are perfectly happy to turn on each other if there is a lack of English types around.

Towards the end of the 2011/2012 season, Rangers FC was facing administration and multiple relegations to the Highlands Fried Mars Bar Division (Under 8s League). In a game against Dundee United, fans pledged their loyalty with 'Rangers till we die. We're Rangers till we die'. Back came the Dundee United fans, perhaps with intimate knowledge of the imminent winding-up order, certainly with knowledge of a winding-up chant – 'Rangers till July! You're Rangers till July! We know you are. You know you are. You're Rangers till July!'

Aldershot fans displayed the same sympathies towards Chester City on the day City were relegated from League Two to the Blue Square Conference in April 2009: 'It's Blue, it's Square, and you're going down to there – Conference, Conference!'

But enough of this negativity. This is the "avin' a laugh' section and the Tartan Army does have a laugh wherever it goes. Unlike too many England fans, they rarely cause trouble when they go away, and they go away everywhere and often. Legend has it that, to this day, there are small pockets of red-haired befreckled men and women, now aged about forty, all the way from Mexico to

Argentina, a legacy of some of the epic journeys made by thousands of Scots who went over for the 1978 World Cup. Large numbers had flown into various American airports and then hitchhiked down through Latin America, having dangerous liaisons along the way.

* * *

Sometimes the banner is mightier than the word. For me the cheeky Scousers came full circle after four decades in the 2013/14 season at Old Trafford.

In 1974, Liverpool played Newcastle in the FA Cup final and thrashed them three–nil in one of the most one-sided finals I can remember. But most memorable that day was the banner held aloft in the Liverpool end in honour of their number seven – Kevin Keegan. It said 'Jesus Saves – But Keegan Gets the Rebound!' Genius. Keegan scored twice that day.

Fast forward to March 2014 and Liverpool are at Old Trafford playing the league champions, Manchester United. The Mancunians are having a terrible time of it: Fergie's gone, David Moyes (former Everton manager) has taken over and is busy overseeing the worst season for the club in two decades. Liverpool go three up and Manchester United's chance of qualifying for the Champions League via the fourth spot in the Premier League is disappearing down a Steve-Gerrard-shaped tunnel. No Champions League place might equal an exodus of talent and a downward spiral; it's serious stuff. So serious that, at this point, the visiting Liverpool fans unfurl a huge banner in the away section saying 'David Moyes Is a Football Genius'. Genius above and way beyond the call of sarcasm. It was professionally made, with a photo of Moyes, printed words, a glossy finish and a Scally flourish.

Contrast that with the pathetic Bayern Munich banner the week before, during their Champions League victory against Arsenal. Two grinning ninnies held up a cheap white cloth banner the size of your kitchen tablecloth, upon which they'd painted a very badly drawn boy that they hoped resembled the Arsenal midfielder, Mesut Özil. Arsenal's nickname is 'The Gunners'. Özil was bending over, away from the cannon, which was firing into his backside. The ensemble was finished off with the words 'Gay Gunners'. Bayern's banner was offensive without even having the caveat of not being malicious. The thought of those two guys at their kitchen table the night before, with a paint pot, brushes and two Löwenbräus is a bit sad.

Liverpool's banner was witty, and may have got under the Manchester United manager's skin, which, along with having a laugh, was the point. A few weeks before, when the pressure was beginning to build on Moyes, Chelsea fans had verbalised the jibe. When their team put in a third goal against Man Utd, they began singing 'We want you to stay. We want you to stay. David Moyes – we want you to stay.' Sadly for Mr Moyes, the Manchester United board didn't agree.

Using banners is more a part of continental European football culture than British, especially in Italy, where a lot of love and attention go into them. They are bright, professional, glossy, but tend not to be particularly humorous. The attitude of British fans is that the odd banner is OK, but that they can be a bit contrived, and the money could be better spent in the pub. Singing.

There are exceptions. The Moyes banner tickled a lot of people's cruel funny bone (that's the one in the middle of your dark heart), and a Man Utd banner from 2012 is worth a mention. Man U had beaten Chelsea in a league match, whereupon

Chelsea did a lot of moaning about the (now fit again) referee Mark Clattenburg. As luck would have it, a few days later they played each other again in a Cup match. United went three–two up, and the fans went ironic and topical with 'Time to blame the referee', but there was icing on the chanting cake.

Chelsea fans have a banner honouring John Terry. It's always up at Stamford Bridge, bearing his name and the tribute 'Captain, Leader, Legend'. After the third goal went in, and the 'Time to blame the referee' chant went up, so did Manchester's banner response to the previous game – 'Clattenburg, Referee, Leader, Legend.' That was a rarity, a printed version of the 'call and response' culture of our songs. The Italians copy, add and reply to their banners; the British copy, add and reply to chants. For example, Man City fans came up with:

This city is ours.
This city is ours.
Fuck off back to London,
This city is ours.

That is a direct challenge to Man Utd, their fan base, and the fact that the club is actually from another city – Salford.

A season later, back come Man Utd with a dig at their neighbours, based on attendances being lower at the Etihad than at Old Trafford:

The city is yours.
The city is yours.
Twenty thousand empty seats,
Are you fucking sure?

Back come City with a dig at their rivals' money problems:

> *U-N-I-T-E-D,*
> *That spells fucking debt to me,*
> *With a knick-knack paddy whack give a dog a bone,*
> *Ocean Finance on the phone!*

OK, if you're going to be childish . . . Man Utd will get personal:

> *You think that your moustache is trendy*
> *You think that your Kicker boots are too*
> *With your Kangol and your fleece*
> *Ben Sherman on for weeks*
> *We know that you're a fucking blue.*

Anyway, the 'Moyes' banner featured heavily on TV and was the subject of many a screen grab and subsequent text and tweet. Fans will not often miss the opportunity to get their point across via the TV. 'Can you hear us on the box?' or 'Are you watching?' is a way of getting at a certain club even when they're not playing your team. And chanting obscenities at a celebrity commentator/analyser on the pitch at half time is considered fun, especially if the celebrity is called Robbie Savage, and disrupting filming can wile away a few minutes before a game starts.

Chesterfield fans excelled at this a decade ago when, for reasons best known to themselves, their club decided to play Partick Thistle up in Glasgow in a pre-season friendly. Scottish Television was recording an episode of Scotland's favourite detective series, *Taggart*. Naturally, Chesterfield's fans decided they preferred a different television detective, perhaps one who was less, say, Scottish.

So the Taggart cameras had to be kept waiting until they had finished their chants of 'One Jack Frost, there's only one Jack Frost . . .'

Once the cameras were switched back on, the Chesterfield fans changed song, feeling it necessary to remind the TV crew about the unfortunate demise of actor Mark McManus, who played Taggart in the 1980s and 90s, by singing 'He's dead. And you know he is'.

Simply appearing on TV is to invite a chant, especially if you are the *Match of the Day* pundit, Alan Shearer. The England great forsook the studio in 2009 in order to manage his beloved Newcastle United in the last eight games of the season, to try to save them from relegation. He took them down amid a ringing in his ears that followed him everywhere he went. It sounded as if people were singing 'Stayed on the telly. You should have stayed on the telly'. Perhaps they were.

''Avin' a laugh' doesn't just involve words. Carrying giant inflatable bananas, or fried eggs, or wearing fancy dress can also be involved. Man City fans claim they started it. This may or may not be true, but they did do it best. According to DaisyCutter.com, the craze was kicked off in the 1987/88 season by a man called Frank Newton, who, for a dare, took a giant inflatable banana to the opening Man City game.

The banana, dressed in a hat with a felt-tip-drawn face, went down very well with fellow supporters who quickly turned a chant about the striker Imre Varadi into 'Imre Banana!' More bananas began to be brought to the ground and then a Frankenstein appeared. He was greeted with a chant of 'Frankie, Frankie'. From there, it was downhill all the way to Surreal City. A dinosaur was brought to one game and began to duel with Frankie above the heads of the crowd. Suddenly a giant inflatable fried egg appeared and it was a three-way fight.

The gloves were off. By the time City played at Stoke on Boxing Day 1998, thousands of the 12,000 travelling City fans were wearing fancy dress costumes and brandishing an inflatable something. The away end was a sea of Batman, Robin, nuns, convicts and brides-to-be waving bananas, crocodiles, penguins and even a giant paddling pool. The City team ran out carrying more giant plastic bananas, which they threw into the crowd. Happy days! By this time fans of other clubs were joining in. Giant inflatable black puddings were served up at Bury, huge plastic haddocks washed up on the terraces at Grimsby.

Inevitably, after a couple of years what was once surreal became normal. It was time to let the air out of the craze. DaisyCutter.com says 'it is difficult to imagine something as gloriously immature as the inflatable craze ever taking off again'. I disagree: football fans are gloriously immature. Give it time.

Whatever the craze is, it won't be celery-shaped, especially at Chelsea. Celery is banned from Stamford Bridge. The club has informed fans: 'If anyone is found attempting to bring celery into Stamford Bridge they could be refused entry and anyone caught throwing celery will face a ban.' Officials even set up a celery hotline so that incidents of celery throwing could be reported.

This followed years of Chelsea fans bringing large sticks of the stuff to games to accompany a song featuring the vegetable and a sex act. Eventually it was being tossed around the stands, which in turn led to it being thrown at the opposing team's players when they took corners. And that was that. Celery got the chop.

No other fans should ever copy celery-throwing; it would be too obvious, too Chelsea. Other clubs' songs do, however, get copied. British clubs nicked the 'Seven Nation Army' tune from the Italians, who had nicked it from a Belgian team, who had nicked it from The

White Stripes. The Italians were all over it in time for Italia 2006. It has now spread across the football world and into other sports.

Borrowing the tune and changing the words is OK, but nicking the tune, the words and the style shows a lack of imagination. The best example of this is the slooooowwwww version of 'Oh When the Spurs Go Marching In' or, rather, 'Oh. When. The. Spurs. (Pause to get coffee) Go. Marching. In. (Pause to read programme notes) Repeat.' It's dire. It's as if the clouds are raining down a barely musical sludge from the heavens. However, what it does have going for it is that when they speed up, it gets better, and is better still when it stops. More importantly, as far I can tell, Spurs fans started it, and if they choose to behave this way, that's up to them. The mystery is why several other Premier League clubs have copied this. Get your own sludge!

*   *   *

Let's end with two songs that sum up what it's all about, unless you're a dour, sour-faced killjoy with no sense of history or fun. The sort of person who just doesn't get that it is precisely because this game we love so much is serious stuff that we shouldn't take it so seriously.

Yes, Bill Shankly said football was 'not a game of life and death – it's more serious than that', but that's because he has a dry sense of humour and was a hard-working man from a tough background who knew that love, life, community, people and family are what it's really all about. He knew football is important to us because Shankly was a football fan. He loved football, and football loved him. He'd have had no time for the death songs, the gloating over people being killed in air crashes or stadium crushes. He would have had no time for a working man who thinks solidarity with his club is displayed by attacking another man in the street.

So let's end on the up. If it's not fun – what's the point? And, yes, that even includes the fun of standing in the rain losing two–nil away in December, because it can still be a laugh.

Shankly was an old-school disciplinarian. He may not have identified with hordes of young men drinking and dancing in the streets, but if he could have seen the video of Man City fans in Madrid, singing the Yaya/Kolo Touré song, he would have understood the sense of away-day togetherness, camaraderie and the sheer exuberance of modern fans. You can see the footage on YouTube if you search for 'Man City Yaya Touré Madrid'.

Yaya and Kolo are brothers who, at the time of the Madrid video, were both in Man City's team. The rhythm in both the words and tune is infectious, the different hand movements in the dancing underline that this is about both brothers, and the whole effect is joyous and slightly surreal. The Touré brothers were once shown the video and both fell about laughing.

In case you can't see it, the song is simply fans outside a bar singing 'Yaya Yaya, Yaya Yaya, Yayayayayaya Touré' accompanied by waving their hands in the air as if at a Born Again American Christian festival. The only other line is 'Kolo Kolo, Kolo Kolo, Kolokolokolo Touré' accompanied by similar hand movements, but this time directed towards the floor while dancing in a manner reminiscent of demonstrators in South Africa.

If you can find the video, watch at about halfway through, for when the older guy (with white hair and wearing a backpack) dances into shot. I'm not sure he even knows the guys he joins, but it matters not, and anyway, he invites the two young Real Madrid fans who are sheepishly dancing at the side to get more involved. He looks as if he's in his mid sixties. Part of me wants to be behaving in a similar manner if I reach that age.

Underneath the video on YouTube are comments. Only a few are derogatory:

- 'Fucking embarrassing, *Soccer AM* fans' – but most clearly get the joy in the moment.
- 'Even as a Chelsea fan, this is my favourite football chant.'
- 'People say its embarrassing but there havin a laugh and a good time aint that what footies about.'
- 'Haha quality some people have a sense of humour by-pass, I think this is quality.'
- 'I like City mate, and I don't begrudge your fans any kind of success one bit, you've had the rough end of the deal for a long time but I'm made up for your fans that you're doing well.'
- 'United fan but this is what football is all about man!!'
- 'Class chant! Even Madrid fans join that's why I love football.'

That's about right. Of course it's also about what happens on the pitch, but the two things go together. For the fans it's not just about the football, it's about all the things that go with it.

With the football, you also get the journey to the ground, you see the architecture of the stadiums, and, more importantly, you get to compare the pies they serve. For the record, Birmingham City's Chicken Balti pies are probably football's finest. You get the beer, the singing, the dancing, the jokes, the laughs, and, even though there should be no crying in football, you get the tears.

You also get the history, which brings us to our closing song. The honour goes to Stockport County. Let's face it, you've got to be a proper football fan to support Stockport County – Football League Division Four Champions 1966–67, three times winners of the

Cheshire Premier Cup (1969–70, 1970–71, 2010–11), and now gracing the Skrill North League. I doubt if any celeb actor chooses County as the team they pretend they've always supported, nor do young boys and girls in Bournemouth grow up wearing blue and white shirts and declaring an undying love for The Hatters.

But the County fans do, and despite the opening line of their anthem – they are not all that is wrong with football (except from time to time in relation to defending crosses).

The song is to the tune of 'The Sash My Father Wore', but the only religious connotation is that you hear it sung in that cathedral of football – Edgeley Park.

> *We are everything in football,*
> *That people say's sad and wrong.*
> *But when we go to Edgeley Park,*
> *We will sing our County songs!*
> *We'll raise our voice in chorus!*
> *As we did in times before.*
> *And at Edgeley Park our greatest pride,*
> *Is the scarf my father wore!*

> Chorus:
> *It's forever being beautiful,*
> *And the colour's white and blue!*
> *I wore it proudly 'round my neck,*
> *At Chesterfield & Crewe!*
> *My father was a County fan,*
> *Like me grandfather before.*
> *And at Edgeley Park I love to wear,*
> *The scarf me father wore!*

We will always follow County,
To all games far and near!
And at Edgeley Park we'll sing those songs,
That me father loved to hear!
We will raise our pints in memory,
Of the games he loved to see.
And at Edgeley Park, I'll wear the scarf,
That me father left to me!

Chorus:
It's passed down the generations,
Of my family!
Oh my granddad gave it to my dad,
And me dad gave it to me.
And when my time is over,
And life's long race is run.
I'll take the scarf from 'round my neck,
And I'll pass it to my son!

It's forever being beautiful,
And the colours white and blue,
I wore the scarf around my neck,
At Chesterfield and Crewe,
My father was a county fan,
Like me grandfather before,
and at Edgeley Park I love to wear,
The scarf my father wore.

There's a lot wrong with football and with fans, but Stockport are part of what is right about both.

In September 2009, County drew two–two away at Yeovil, and that's a long way away. Both Stockport goals were scored by Carl Baker. The game was on a Saturday. On the Thursday, the then manager Gary Ablett had broken the news to Baker that his older brother, Michael, had died of leukaemia. At the time, Baker's younger brother, Dean, was also suffering from cancer.

Later, after taking in the news, Baker phoned Ablett and insisted he was available to make the 400-mile round trip down to Yeovil and, if picked, was fit to play. When he scored the first goal, Ablett, and others on the bench, produced a T-shirt saying 'For U Mike' which Baker held aloft as all ten other team members gathered around him.

At the end of the game, the midfielder was walking back to the tunnel when Ablett stopped him and sent him over to the 200 or so County fans who had been singing his name throughout the game. In the pubs beforehand, a card had been handed round for as many of the travelling supporters as possible to sign before it was sent to the player and his family. Others queued up on the terraces to put notes inside it. After they handed over the card, tears and hugs were exchanged between player and fans. The emotional scenes continued in the dressing room.

The Baker family story was one of the reasons Stockport County had gone into a commercial partnership with Leukaemia Research. After Michael's death, the financially challenged club auctioned off team shirts bearing the Leukaemia Research logo to raise more money for the charity. They also gave it free advertising space at Edgeley Park, and the players, staff and fans freely gave of their time to promote the cause. The family had come together.

That's football.

Acknowledgements

Thanks to Matthew Bayley (Spurs), Enda Brady (Ireland, 'I've given up on club football'), Martin Brunt (Gillingham), Franklin Marshall Collins ('You don't mean magnetic you mean temporal when it comes to Fergie's space and time'), Grace Marshall Collins ('I deserve a name check for having to listen to you singing football songs'), Jo Marshall Collins (QPR), Ollie Dewis (Villa), Lew Dias (Arsenal), Peter Diapre (Southampton 'Till I die'), Ben Freeman (Leeds), Nathan Hale (Bristol Rovers), Phil Hardacre (Leeds), Eamonn Holmes (Man Utd), Ronan Hughes (Man Utd), Tom Kelly (Elgar Society, Rovers), Mark Kleinman (Charlton), Andrew Lindsay (Man Utd), Me (Leeds), Thomas Moore (Forest), Peter Oborne (Cricket, dear boy), Paul (Man City), Lee Petar (Man Utd), Ashley Rolfe (Chelsea), Grant Smith (Chelsea), Mark E. Smith (Sparta FC), Nigel Spackman (Bournemouth, Chelsea, Liverpool, Queens Park Rangers, Rangers, Chelsea, Sheffield United), Nick Stylianou ('Man Utd, from Surrey, but my uncle's from Stockport, I promise'), Craig Summers (West Ham), Anwar Tambe (Luton,'The Mighty Hatters'), Dave Terris (West Ham 'season ticket holder – problem is it faces the pitch'), Jolly Thompson (Villa), Phil Wardman (Derby), Glenn Weatherall (Millwall), Hugh Westbrook (Brentford).

These are just some of the sources used for this book:
Jack Bremner, *Shit Ground No Fans*, Bantam Press, 2004
Anthony Clavane, *Does Your Rabbi Know You're Here? The Story of English Football's Forgotten Tribe*, Quercus, 2012

"Dirty Northern Bastards!"

God, Exodus, Mount Sinai Press, 1446 BCE

Stuart Maconie, *Pies and Prejudice: In Search of the North,* Ebury Press, 2008

Gershon Portnoi, *Who Are Ya? Football's Best Ever Chants*, Simon and Schuster, 2011

Max Velody, *Can We Play You Every Week? A Journey to the Heart of All 92 Football League Clubs*, Short Books, 2008

Paul Winslow, *Songs from the Barmy Army*, Simon and Schuster, 2012

Song Credits

p. 17: chant based on the lyrics to 'Do They Know It's Christmas' by Bob Geldof and Midge Ure. Published by Chappell Music Ltd. **p. 18:** chant based on the lyrics to 'Thank U Very Much' by Michael McGear. Published by Universal Music Publishing Group. **pp. 38–39:** 'In My Liverpool Home' by Pete McGovern and the Spinners. Published by Spin Publications. **p. 43** and **p. 44**: chants based on the lyrics to *The Addams Family* theme tune by Vic Mizzy, Marc Shaiman. Published by Next Decade Entertainment O.B.O. Unison Music Company, Unison Music, Famous Music LLC, Unison Music Company. **p. 64:** 'The Hartlepool Monkey' by Alan Wilkinson. Reproduced with permission. **p. 65:** chant based on the lyrics to 'Who Let The Dogs Out' by Anselm Douglas. Published by BMG Rights Management. **p. 73**: chant based on the lyrics to 'Chim Chim Cher-ee' from *Mary Poppins* by Robert B. Sherman & Richard M. Sherman. Copyright Wonderland Music Company, Inc. **p. 77:** chant based on the lyrics to 'Always Look On The Bright Side Of Life' by Eric Idle. Published by Kay-Gee-Bee Music Ltd and EMI Virgin Music Ltd. **p. 78**: chant based on the lyrics to 'I Bet You Look Good on the Dance Floor' by Alex Turner. Published by EMI Music Publishing Ltd. **pp. 84–85:** 'Keep Right on to the End of the Road'. Written by Will Dillon and Harry Lauder. Published by EMI Music Publishing Ltd/Francis Day and Hunter Ltd and © Harms Inc – Redwood Music Ltd in respect of the 50% interest o/b/o the Estate of William A Dillon – All Rights Reserved – Used by Permission. **p. 87**: chant based on the lyrics to 'Mull of Kintyre' by Paul McCartney and Denny Laine. Published by MPL Communications Ltd. **pp. 88–89:** 'The Fields of Athenry' composed by Pete St. John. Published by Celtic Songs and Pete St. John. **p. 92**: chant based on the lyrics to 'All You Need Is Love' by John Lennon and Paul McCartney. Copyright Sony/ATV Music Publishing LLC. **p. 99** and **p. 100**: chants based on the lyrics to 'Annie's Song' by John Denver. Published by Cherry Lane Music Publishing Company Inc. and DreamWork Songs. **p. 111**: translated song based on 'Blue Is the Colour' by D Boone, S Houston and R McQueen. Published by Page One Records. **p. 112:** 'Blue Moon' lyrics by Lorenz Hart. Published by EMI Robbins Catalog, Inc. Lyrics © Sony/ATV Music Publishing LLC. **p. 114**: chant based on the lyrics to

Acknowledgements

'Singing the Blues' by Melvin Endsley. Published by Fort Knox Music Inc., Sony/ATV Acuff Rose Music, MusiXmatch. **pp. 118–19**: 'Leeds, Leeds, Leeds (Marching On Together)'. Words by Barry Mason. Music by Les Reed. © Copyright 1972 Dick James Music Limited. Universal/Dick James Music Limited. All Rights Reserved. International Copyright Secured. Used by permission of Music Sales Limited. **p. 121**: 'Glory Glory Leeds United' by Ronnie Hilton. Traditional arrangement. Produced by Walter J. Ridley. EMI Publishing 1968. **p. 127**: 'Honolulu Wednesday' based on 'Honolulu Baby' by Thomas Marvin Hartley. Published by Robert Kingston (Music) Ltd. **pp. 131–32**: 'Goodnight Irene' by Huddie Ledbetter/John Lomax. © 1936 (renewed 1964) and 1950 Ludlow Music, Inc., USA assigned to TRO Essex Music Ltd of Suite 2.07, Plaza 535, King's Road, London SW10 0SZ. International Copyright Secured. All Rights Reserved. Used by Permission. **p. 136–37**: 'Steve Bloomer's Watching' by Mark Tewson and Martin Miller. Published by Bucks Music Group Ltd. **p. 142**: chant based on the lyrics to 'The Bells Are Ringing' by Betty Comden, Adolph Green and Jule Styne. Published by Warner/Chappell Music Inc. **p. 145**: 'All Together Now' written by Peter Hooton/Steve Grimes. Published by Union Square Music Songs Ltd. **pp. 147–48**: 'Sunshine on Leith' by Charles Stobo Reid and Craig Morris Reid. © Warner/Chappell Music Ltd (PRS). All Rights Reserved. **p. 151**: chant based on the lyrics to 'Anarchy in the UK' by Glen Matlock and John Lydon. Published by A Thousand Miles Long, Inc., Warner/Chappell Music Ltd, Universal Music – Careers, Rotten Music Ltd. **p. 165**: chant based on the lyrics to 'Eleanor Rigby' by John Lennon and Paul McCartney. Copyright Sony/ATV Music Publishing LLC. **p. 166**: chant based on the lyrics to 'Blame it on the Boogie' by Mick Jackson, Dave Jackson and Elmar Krohn. Published by Chrysalis Music Group. **p. 166**: chant based on the lyrics to 'Happy Days' theme tune by Norman Gimbel and Charles Fox. Published by BSX Records. **p. 167**: chant based on the lyrics to 'Love Will Tear Us Apart' by Ian Curtis, Peter Hook, Stephen Morris and Bernard Sumner. Published by Zomba Music Publishers Ltd. **p. 168**: chant based on the lyrics to 'Pass the Dutchie' by Marlin Greene and Eddie Hinton. Published by Warner/Chappell Music Inc. **p. 169**: chant based on the lyrics to 'Oh My God' by Nicholas Hodgson, Richard Wilson, Andrew White, James Rix and Nicholas Baines. Copyright Imagem Music. **p. 169**: chant based on the lyrics to 'No Limits' by Myron Lavell Avant, Filip de Wilde, Anita D. Doth, Jean-Paul Henriette de Coster, Raymond Slijngaard, Stephen Edward Huff. Published by Decos, Grindtime Publishing, Songs Of Universal Inc., Universal Music – Z Songs, Decos Publishing, Tuff Huff Music LLC. **p. 170**: chant based on the lyrics to 'Wonderwall' by Noel Gallagher. Published by Sony/ATV Music Publishing. **p. 170**: chant based on the lyrics to 'Another Brick in the Wall' by Roger Waters. Published by Roger Waters Music Overseas Ltd. **p. 187**: chants based on the lyrics to 'Don't You Want Me Baby' written by Phil Oakey, Phil Wright and Jo Callis. Published by EMI Records Ltd. **p. 187**: chant based on the lyrics to 'Radio Ga Ga' by Roger Taylor. Copyright Queen Music Ltd.

Index

Index

Index

Index